No Limits

No Limits

The powerful true story of Leah Goldstein:
World Kickboxing Champion,
Israeli Undercover Police
and Cycling Champion.

Leah Goldstein
with
Lori Friend Moger

Editor: Nina Shoroplova
Assistant Editor: Susan Kehoe
Production Editor: Jennifer Kaleta
Typeset: Greg Salisbury
Portrait Photographers: Jeff Bassett, Heath Fletcher
Cover photographer: Dina Goldstein
Book Cover Design: Liz Stanley

DISCLAIMER: This is a work of non-fiction. The names of some individuals in this book have been changed. This is a personal story. The activities in this book are not described for the purposes of recommending them to the reader. Readers of this publication agree that neither Leah Goldstein, nor her publisher will be held responsible or liable for damages that may be alleged or resulting directly or indirectly from their use of this publication. All external links are provided as a resource only and are not guaranteed to remain active for any length of time. Neither the publisher nor the author can be held accountable for the information provided by, or actions resulting from accessing these resources.

From Leah:
For my grandmother, Frieda, who always told me to
never use the words "I wish."

From Lori:
For Cam and Halle whom I hope always know that
life is just an adventure.

Testimonials

"I always knew Leah Goldstein was hardcore but this book takes any notion I had to a whole other level. This is an incredible story of a life lived from the heart of a champion. Leah shows that nothing is impossible and I just cannot believe she is real. If you want to be inspired and realize there is nothing standing between you and your dreams, read this book."

Clara Hughes, O.C.
6-Time Olympic Medalist

"Leah's incredible story will have you questioning everything you thought you knew about human potential. Her life elevates all of us, and forces a new definition of the word 'limit'! A must read for all of us who dare to dream big ...."

George Thomas
Race Across America Finish Line Announcer, Race Across Oregon, Double Trouble, Ring of Fire Director and The Natchez Trace 444 Director

"I couldn't put this book down. Leah Goldstein tells an incredibly compelling story of how she came to be a champion athlete. No Limits is a fascinating look at extreme motivation and guts."

Joe Friel
Cofounder of Training Peaks and Author of
The Triathelete's Training Bible.

"No Limits *is a fascinating and informative true story that takes you on a journey into the heart and mind of a champion athlete to reveal how she was able to conquer challenges that could have crushed her spirit. Leah's lessons and honest writing show you how to go the extra mile in your sport and life."*

Dr. Jim Afremow

Ph.D., Author of *The Champion's Mind: How Great Athletes Think, Train, and Thrive*

Contents

INTRODUCTION

In my life as a speaker, I get the opportunity to listen to many other professionals trying to motivate and inspire their audiences. "Intentional Thinking" and "Aligning Your Inner Energy" are hot topics right now, as most people seem to want to find a switch or an easy button that will turn their lives around. It's not as though I don't believe that those things have some effect, but they all seem to discount the main cause of success. That awful four-letter word that generationally we seem to be forgetting how to do: work. Work! By nature, however, humans are attracted to passive goal-setting and habits. That's what's in our DNA.

Doesn't it sound much easier to write what you want on your bathroom mirror, rather than actually going out and getting it done? Trust me, if you put an escalator in the middle of Kenya, where some of the fiercest and fittest human warriors still reside, they would use it. Maasai warriors hunt hyenas and can jump four feet in the air, but they would still use the escalator. Why?

It's in our genes. We're supposed to conserve energy when possible, expending only when absolutely necessary. And up until about a hundred years ago, it was very necessary. People worked, physically. At their jobs and at home, people burned their calories in an effort to *live*. Now, surrounded by dishwashers and low-maintenance yards, we kick back and enjoy the stillness that technology offers. Could it be that this sedation has spilled over into our spirit, our dreams, and our character?

I think a worthwhile life requires movement—physically, mentally, spiritually. Our belief systems and values need exercise, challenges, and change. Competing in ultra-distance cycling allowed me to test all of these things, while offering up eleven long days of uninterrupted reflection of my life. I tend to be extreme by nature, so I'm not suggesting everyone head out and start jogging across Texas. But I believe we are all greater human beings when we seek situations that stretch our minds, bodies, and souls. After all, it's the only way to truly discover what's possible.

The 3,000-mile Race Across America (RAAM, the "M" left in there for America) lures the crazy/brave (it's a fine line) crowd, those people who simply must test their limits in order to feel alive. I entered for many reasons, including that one. I had only two goals in mind: 1. To win; and 2. To break the record. The race is insanely expensive and requires a full year of training and logistical preparations.

Each solo rider needs two follow vehicles, several bikes, spare parts, tools, lots of clothes, coolers, packaged food, and a diverse crew. My parents tagged along for the trip in their own vehicle, plus my friend Janessa acted as crew chief, handling much of the planning. Another friend, Lori helped with much of the prep work too, and brought aboard her sister, Connie (a triathlete from Michigan) and her buddy, Rob (a paramedic). My long-time friend Ed, who had served as our mechanic when I rode for the Canadian

National Team, agreed to come along to take care of the bicycles, as did Sean, a young guy who worked on my gear in my new hometown of Vernon, British Columbia (B.C.). We rented a minivan as our follow car, the vehicle allowed to leapfrog me throughout the race (and follow right behind me at night, providing safety and more light). Two crewmembers would work an eight-hour shift in the car, handing me bottles of liquid and food, fixing bike problems, helping me to the bathroom, and navigating the thousands of turns on route. The rest of the crew rode in my dad's RV and prepped food, planned potential rest points, and slept.

Just as in professional races, I wore an earpiece, taped into my right ear. My follow car could talk to me anytime, and by pressing a small button on the connecting wire, I could speak to them. The little earbud became more and more important as the race went on and my crew had to keep me awake, alert me to traffic, and tell me when to stop. Ceding control of a situation was a foreign experience for me. I had to rely on them to push me, feed me, and keep me awake and away from danger. But they all rose to the challenge and were a crucial component of my success.

I used RAAM as a testing ground, a final battlefield to see what I was made of. *How much can I take?* I expected to come away euphoric and proud—how could one not be after tackling such a race? But what I received was so much more than that, for in the most blaring, painful moments I could actually feel my mind slowing down, quieting. The long, repetitive days allowed my normally racing thoughts to subdue, just enough to let my conscious brain hear what's really important. My own inner voice finally told me what I really needed to hear.

Race Across America's 3,000-mile route includes 170,000 feet of climbing.

Oceanside, California

"One day, your life will flash before your eyes. Make sure it's worth watching."

Unknown

Breathe. My stomach is a knot. Did I even eat breakfast this morning? I suddenly can't remember. Am I really going to start a 3,000-mile bike race without eating breakfast? What would my Jewish-and-constantly-trying-to-feed-the-world mother say? Just breathe, dammit, and focus.

"And hailing from Canada, a National Champion, multiple race record holder and twelve-year pro cyclist, Leah Goldstein!" George, the Race Across America Director, calls me to the line. A few claps and cheers went up, but all I could hear was my heart pounding.

"Now this girl is something else! Brand new to the ultra-cycling world last year, and she's been untouchable!"

Oh, crap, please don't jinx me.

"Winner of Furnace Creek and Race Across Oregon, here she is attempting her first RAAM race—and believe me, she won't be satisfied with anything but first place!"

That's actually true ... can we please just start?

The RAAM starting line in Oceanside, California is a cluster of RVs, team vans, nervous crewmembers, and lots of bikes. The non-stop 3,000 mile race started in 1982 by a couple of insane (I mean that in the nicest way) cyclists who just wanted to see who could get

1

from L.A. to the Empire State Building first. John Marino, who also raced, organized the event. John Howard, Lon Haldeman, and Michael Shermer rounded out the field of four. Remember that last name "Shermer"; it will be important later.

The rules of the race have hardly varied in its thirty-two-year history. The gun goes off, and the first person to get to the finish line wins. That's it. Most of the racers would start on Saturday, four days from my start day, in the team division. There are two-, four-, and eight-man (and/or woman) teams. And the men's solo riders wouldn't start for another twenty-four hours. But that day, a Tuesday, a mere five solo women and fourteen senior men would head east to the Atlantic.

Caroline van den Bulk, my only age-group competitor, wheeled her Trek up next to me. My crew had told me that she had trained all winter in South America, had a pimped-out RV, and fully paid crew. *Who knows if that's really true?* I sat on a trainer all winter in Canada, had a forty-year old RV that we weren't really sure would make it across the county, let alone the country, and a ragtag crew of friends and friends of friends. Caroline had also already attempted RAAM, and though she'd fallen short by a few states, she knew things I didn't.

I can't lose sight of this one.

"Nice Trek," she smiled, looking my bike up and down, as I did the same to hers.

Cyclists are snobs. We check out each other's bikes; the components, wheels, seat, everything. It's ridiculous, but we can't help ourselves. My Trek was awesome, although without the same high-end electronic shifting that she had. You know when you have to pull or push a lever to shift gears on your bike? Yeah, she just pushes a button. That's the kind of stuff that makes cyclists beyond happy. It's a curse.

"Yeah, you too," I replied.

"You ready for this? Do you know what you've gotten yourself into?" she smiled.

"Yeah, I think so," I forced a laugh.

"I had to pull out last time because of severe dehydration. It happens a lot, so watch out for that. This race is crazy. You won't believe what will happen to you out there."

So I've heard. Ex-racers warned me about the hallucinations, falling asleep on the bike, saddle sores, and sickness. In fact, George our Race Director joked at our team meeting yesterday, "It's not a matter of if you'll get sick, but when."

I wasn't afraid of any of that, really. I was afraid of the unknown. *Would this be the life event that would finally crack me? Could I actually completely breakdown, mentally or physically, and be unable to finish?* I had been a pro racer for over twelve years, but with only a couple of ultra-distance events for experience, I was a complete novice. I knew what happens to your body after thirty hours or forty-eight hours of hard racing. But beyond that, I really didn't know.

Few people attempt RAAM as a solo rider, the solo field averaging only about twenty-six riders each year. Even fewer finish—in a normal year over half the solo field drops out.

"Did you know more people climbed Mt. Everest last year, than have ever finished this race?" a grey-haired guy winked at me.

"Really? That's comforting," I managed. *It's also 50 percent longer than the Tour de France, and we have half the time to finish it.*

This was his third attempt at RAAM, having failed within 200 miles of the finish last year. I tried to imagine pedaling for ten or eleven days and not making the finish. My stomach hardened. *I would have to be nearly dead to drop out of this race.*

"Well, I'm sure you'll do fine. You're quite a rider."

I didn't have the heart to tell him he was one of the few cyclists who seemed confident in the possibility of me winning RAAM. Most ultra-distance athletes had warned me of "too much too soon." It usually takes a few years of "shorter" distance races, like 500 to 800 miles, to build up the endurance in your body. Ultra cycling is not just about pedaling for a long time. Your joints, muscles, digestive system, and yes, unmentionables, must adjust to the constant work. I had completed just three ultra races in the past year, but was too impatient to wait another year. Or more probable, I wasn't sure I wanted to sacrifice another entire year endlessly training on my bike. For the third time in my life, I felt ready to start a new chapter.

My thoughts quickly spun back to the starting line. I rolled my wheel up to the banner while George read the rest of my bio. My mother, father, and seven crewmembers lined the starting chute, leaning over the metal barriers clapping and taking pictures. In slow motion, the gun went off and I pushed forward into the unknown. Veterans of the race had told me that as the race went on, my thoughts would become more and more scattered; events that had only stood out for a moment as a child would suddenly rear up and make me sad or angry or afraid all over again.

As I pedaled out of the hazy beach town, I dreaded the stories of my past that I didn't want to think about. *I don't want to relive that terrifying moment. I don't want to remember that lonely time.* But the memories did come. Pedaling along a plain white line for eleven days straight, they bombarded me with no mercy. I took them as they came, watching my life play out in front of me, as if trapped in a theatre with no exit.

When I had told my friend, Lori, that I was planning to do Race Across America, she asked me something no one else ever had.

"What are you running from?" At first, I thought she was kidding, but I saw that she had her psychology face on.

"I don't know."

"Yes, you do."

I'm used to people asking me "why," and I have a great repertoire of snappy comebacks that seems to appease them.

"I've always wanted to do this race."

"What else am I going to do with myself?"

"Because it's there."

But the reason isn't that simple. While most people would be afraid to take on a race like this, I was scared not to. Scared of the ordinary—of being normal. Disappearing. My entire life, I've been the girl who everyone watches to see what crazy thing will happen next. I feared that if I stopped racing, I would lose part of myself. That thing that pumps me full of adrenaline and makes me feel alive would be lost and I'd never be the same. Competition was like my best friend, and I wasn't ready to lose it.

When faced with fear, we think we have two choices: fight or flight. That's right, isn't it? I mean, that's what our high school biology teachers told us. Our adrenal glands fire high levels of cortisol and adrenaline into our blood stream, which increases our heart rate and blood pressure. Our body is "loading" (or "prepping") to either run away from the perceived danger, or fight for our lives. It's old hardware, granted, and developed from thousands of years of being chased by wolves and tigers. In our modern world, the system seems obsolete—ridiculous even. What do we need to run from now? Or fight for? Certainly very few life-or-death situations present themselves to any of us during our eighty-something years on earth.

Therefore, I believe, many of us have fallen into a third,

and much more dangerous choice when faced with perceived fear. We freeze. We do nothing, and, therefore, neither have to risk failure nor success. I'm continually surprised by my audiences' reaction to my story; as, to me, it's just my journey and nothing more. I think people find my life fascinating simply because I've never, ever, been frozen.

I've simply never stopped, and if that's all people get out of my story, I'll be satisfied. To move, do, explore, and change, instead of sitting, planning, worrying, and drowning in apathy. Have I made bad decisions? You bet. Big ones. But bad choices beat no choice every time, because they are still movement. And I'm here to remind you that more often than not, a risky decision could turn into an incredible change for the better, couldn't it? Or taking a long-shot gamble could very well be the biggest win of your life.

Let's just talk about it right up front. I am afraid. I've been afraid of many things since childhood, the list ebbing and changing throughout my life. You may find it strange, that someone like me would be afraid of anything. I've faced most peoples' worst fears—like terrible injuries, public speaking, and death, and while the thought of those things makes me nervous, none of them are so scary as to stop me from moving forward.

As a child, however, I often felt myself creeping close to that edge of freezing. I was terrified—of the dark, being kidnapped, monsters, and strangers. Mostly kids' stuff, but my shy, sensitive nature compounded everything. I wasn't just wary of strangers. I looked at them from behind my mother's leg and imagined all the mean and terrible things they may be capable of, and then planned the amazing and high-tech ways I could escape if they tried to take me. A petrified James Bond. I know, it's a paradox, but try to stay with me.

I was especially afraid of God. My mom's cousins took me to their ultra-Christian church a few times, a foreign place where people spoke in tongues and washed each other's feet. My family was Jewish, observing holidays and keeping a moderately kosher kitchen, but we rarely went to synagogue. I knew who God was, and the basic Old Testament stories, but this Christian church brought God and his wrath to a whole new level. One Sunday, the congregation watched a movie, where Satan, a bad angel as I recall, came to earth and gave people a choice. Either they could live out their life however they chose, and when they died, their soul would become his property, or they could accept Jesus as their savior and get beheaded right then and there.

The parents in the film were comforting their children as they waited in line for the chopping block.

"Don't worry, Johnny. We will all be together in heaven," the mom said, patting a kid my age on the back.

He put his little neck in a guillotine, the blade sliced down, and his brown-haired head fell into a black bucket. One by one, the Jesus people sacrificed their lives for eternal life in heaven. I was horrified. Tears sprang to my eyes as I scanned the faces of the congregation. Surely this wasn't real? Was it? My cousin just rubbed my back.

"You don't have to worry, Leah. All you have to do is pray to Jesus, and you will get to go to heaven."

So I did. Not out of love or anything spiritual. It was complete fear. I performed my daily prayers while I did my ten minutes of sit-ups each night. I'm not sure why I started this routine, although I probably heard sit-ups make you stronger, and, therefore, did them on my own from the age of seven. Each night, I'd tuck my toes under the end of the couch, make sure no one was around (it was secret; again, I don't know why), and start a stopwatch.

1-2-3-4-5. *Please Jesus, forgive my family that doesn't believe in you.* 6-7-8-9-10. *Please make my sick dog better and keep the bullies away from me at school.* 11-12-13-14-15. *Oh, and please don't make me get my head chopped off. Amen.*

My older sister Iris and I often spent the night with our cousins, and our parents would pick us up Sunday morning. If they were late, we'd end up in a pew. A few visits later, my father was waiting outside the church. His red face and clenched fists were enough of a message for my cousins—they'd never be late again. They weren't, and I never went back to that church, but I continued to pray to Jesus. Just in case.

In the midst of early teenage rebellion, Iris saw every scary movie, rode every crazy ride, and jumped into cars with questionable teenage drivers, all while grudgingly dragging me along.

My parents worked overtime to pay the bills, and

my sister was often left to babysit me. We saw *Jaws* and *Halloween* and *Nightmare on Elm Street*, rode the rickety wooden roller coaster at Playland in Vancouver, and peeled down 16th Street in a souped-up Camaro. To my thirteen-year old sister, this was what made life worth living. To me, at nine, it was completely terrifying. After seeing *Jaws*, I couldn't stay in the bathroom for more than twenty seconds, convinced that the huge shark would find its way up the plumbing and eat me. *Fight or flight?*

At night, lying in the dark, my imagination ran wild. *What if a kidnapper puts a pillow over my face and I can't scream? What if Jason in the goalie mask jumps out of my closet? If I hear splashing in the toilet, I'm going out the window.* I never had a night light as a child, although, embarrassingly enough, I have one now. I would stay awake after my mother tucked me into bed, and I could hear my sister's soft breathing, and then sneak to the bathroom and turn on the light. Most nights, with the reassuring glow from the hallway, I was able to finally close my eyes. But some nights, I would stare at the hallway until midnight. I'd take my blanket and pillow, and sneak into my parents' room and sleep on the floor beside my mother. I'd wake up early and slide back into my own bed, never wanting my sister to tease me or my mother to worry.

Throughout early elementary school, I felt like an outsider. I barely knew the English alphabet, and putting the letters together into sounds baffled me. While other kids raised their hands and volunteered to read out loud or write on the board, I sat in the back row and tried to disappear. I observed as my classmates played dress-up and colored and sewed buttons on cards. I could not for the life of me understand why any of that was fun. I sat alone and watched.

I avoided speaking whenever possible, my lisp and poor English making me an easy target for teasing. I grew up in a household that spoke mostly Hebrew, but even that was a second language for my parents. Their English was even worse. They spoke to each other in a mix of Hebrew, Russian, and English, depending on the topic and how much they wanted my sister and me to understand. My parents did a lot of language swapping back then, assuming the Russian discussion about bills and groceries was just between them. I listened and spied so much though that I could understand most of what they were saying, no matter which language they slipped into.

They were non-English speaking immigrants with two children, trying to carve a life out in a tough Canadian economy. My parents had immigrated from Israel in 1968 when my sister was four and my mother pregnant with me. My father was lucky to find work as a welder just after arriving. His co-workers used to joke with him, "Who ever heard of a Jewish guy working down on the floor?" He would laugh along and nod—but it was only about a year later when he opened his own welding business and all those guys were working for him.

My father loved to live up to the stereotypical Jewish businessman. He cared about one thing—security for his family—and no one worked harder than he did. My mother was a trained nurse, but because of the language barrier, she could only secure work at a Jewish old age home. They both had a series of high-demand, low-paying jobs in those early years. I could hear the strain in their Russian-speaking voices as they discussed finances and missing their families. When they'd notice me eavesdropping, they'd switch back to their soft-sounding Hebrew and ask if I wanted some food. Always food. So Jewish.

My parents bought and sold houses to earn extra money. My father would spot a bargain house and we'd move in. They'd fix it up (nothing major, we weren't exactly handy people) and resell it. My family moved ten times before I turned seventeen, so my journey to school changed often, sometimes a few blocks and sometimes five kilometers away. I had two choices. Take the city bus or ride my bike. There was no contest—I loved my bike. The longer the commute, the better. I would time myself from driveway to driveway, always trying to corner sharper and climb hills faster.

The daredevil in me kept growing and I looked for more risks, while the rest of me grew more shy and withdrawn. Getting a shot of euphoria from a hard bike ride each morning made walking into my classroom each morning a bit easier. I always tried to get to school early so I wouldn't have to enter the classroom with everyone watching me. I had no close childhood friends, until I met Matthew.

Matthew was in my class at Emily Carr Elementary School. He was a small kid, with straw-straight red hair and more freckles than you could count. I guess we started hanging out because none of the other kids wanted to. We both got picked on, but together we felt safer. We rode bikes, played war at recess, and started a very risky lunchtime adventure. It started on a rare, sunny Vancouver spring day. We decided to walk to 7-Eleven and steal some candy. Leaving school grounds was forbidden, of course, and shoplifting illegal; but we convinced ourselves that we were such good spies we'd never get caught. It was almost too easy to slip through the bushes and run across West 21st Avenue and browse the candy aisle. The store was always busy, and rarely had more than one person working. We'd grab two bags full of Sour Patch Kids and Gummy Bears, shove them up our sleeves and into our pockets, and walk out.

It was a blast, and we went "shopping" every few days for weeks. That is, until Matthew's hidden candy bag dropped right in front of the sales clerk. I saw it start to inch down his sleeve, but before I could warn him, the bag plunked onto the linoleum. The sales lady started yelling at him as she ran around the counter. "You stay right there! You are in big trouble little boy!"

Matthew froze and I just kept walking. I acted casual, pretended I didn't know him, and slunk out the front door.

I felt guilty for ditching him, but my fear of getting caught overwhelmed me, and I continued back to school. I stopped only twice—once to look behind me, positive someone would be running after me, and once to dump the evidence from my pockets into a trashcan. I waited in the playground for the cops to come and arrest me, but instead, not far behind me, came Matthew. The sales lady had let him go with a stern warning, and he had refused to tell her that I stole, too. I couldn't believe he'd covered for me—and for the first time, I felt like I had a true friend.

Unfortunately, Matthew and I couldn't escape the bullying. One kid in our class, Jason, used to convince his friends to chase us on the playground. They may have thought it was a harmless game, but as they yelled, "There they are—chase them!" and "We're gonna get you!"—we ran, completely terrified.

Looking back, I guess we were easy targets. My terrible English and Matthew's Raggedy Andy hair were just too much fun to pick on. They caught Matthew one day and shoved him hard. I remember feeling small and powerless, as he slowly got back up and brushed off his clothes.

Before the end of Grade 2, however, I'd had enough. I was running at top speed away from Jason and his cronies, when I just stopped and spun around on him. *If he's going to beat me up, then today is the day. I'm just not going to run anymore.* He stopped in his tracks, shocked to see me facing him. I started spewing insults as fast as I could. "If you're so tough, then let's see it. But just know, that I'm going to kick the crap out of you! And the whole school will find out what a sissy you really are when you get beat up by a girl!"

I was totally lying, of course. I didn't feel tough at all. But that day was a turning point. I felt a fire light in me that I hadn't ever experienced before. I realized that I could control a situation, just with my energy. If I was tough, then I wouldn't be picked on. If I was strong, then everyone else would respect me. If I was a fighter, then people would describe me as "the athletic one," rather than the small Jewish girl who couldn't speak English.

That's when the obsession started.

It got even worse years later (wait for it). But that's when I started asking my parents for tae kwon do lessons. And I'm talking every-single-day asking. It seemed a perfect fit for me. I would be able to defend my friends and myself from playground bullies, and I could start to transform myself into my idol, Bruce Lee.

From the time I was very young, I was completely fanatical about the kung fu movie star. I was six years old the first time I saw a scene from one of his movies, and I was hooked. I couldn't believe such a small man could take down huge bad guys so effortlessly. I watched his interviews, movies, and anything else I could get my hands on. Once a week, my father would take me to the movie rental store and let me get anything I wanted. I couldn't wait for Saturdays, to walk through those double doors and beeline straight to the action film aisle. I'd meet my father back at the front with Bruce Lee in hand. And he'd always comment something like, "What? Why you want to watch such a junky movie?" in his clipped Hebrew accent. He always gave in, though, and I'd tuck the video under my arm in victory. He was right—the movies were cheaply made and often poor quality. But I didn't care a bit. Bruce Lee was fighting, and I was watching.

So when I started asking about lessons, I thought I'd start

the next day. But my mother was really concerned about my legs and told me I would have to wait. My right leg had never been quite right—in fact, it was a good inch shorter than my left and much weaker. I fell down the stairs when I was three years old, and as my mother was checking me out for injuries—she noticed it. It shocked her enough that she took me right to the doctor. The only conclusion he could offer was that I was born that way and I would probably have trouble with it until adulthood. He was right. For years, I would spend my evenings crying from the pain in my leg. My mother would make me soak it in Epsom salts and hot water. It helped—sometimes.

As I got older, I would have more good days than bad, but the pain persisted into my late teens. I was an incredibly active kid though, and refused to let my leg interrupt my busy outdoor schedule. From morning until dinner, I was at the park, on my bike, climbing trees, and getting dirty. But my mother was wary of my leg, and wanted it to be stronger before I started any organized sports.

She said I could start when I was nine, and that was the end of that.

I suspect now, that another factor may have been money, although my parents would never admit that. The first few years in Canada were difficult for them and sometimes the tension was so thick I could see it in the air.

Just before my big ninth birthday (I worshipped Bruce Lee now more than ever), we suddenly moved from our three-bedroom house in the suburbs into a small one-bedroom apartment in Vancouver. I was too young to understand exactly what was happening, although old enough to see the strain in my parents' faces. No one discussed exactly what had happened, but it seemed as though the hard work of the past ten years had just vanished, and we were right back to the beginning.

Suddenly money was tight again, but my parents did their best to keep us feeling like it wasn't. Throughout that time, my mother really became my best friend. I was extremely serious as a child, and found I enjoyed hanging out with my mother more than with anyone else. She made everything an adventure and filled the role of playmate for much of my young life.

Our four-story apartment building was a depressing yellow color, and only allowed adults. My mother had told me that we were lucky to have this place, since the manager had made an exception for us. I didn't feel lucky. My sister and I shared the bedroom at the end of the hall, and my parents slept on the pull-out couch. I'm only assuming that's what happened because they never pulled it out before we went to bed, and it was all put away by the time we got up.

I tried to feel grateful, just like my mother told me, but I could only roll my eyes and hold my breath as I wheeled my bike into the dank entryway. The manager came out of his first floor apartment, just as I was hoisting my bike to carry it up the stairs. He slid between me and the first step, his hands shoved deep into the pockets of his brown trousers. I took a quick glance at his thick black hair and swollen nose. His pointy shoes peeked out from beneath his bell-bottoms. I immediately decided he was probably in the Greek mafia. I had a bad feeling before he even opened his mouth.

"You can't take bikes into the apartment."

I lowered my red and black BMX bike slowly to the floor, waiting for him to make another exception. The chrome still gleamed with right-out-of-the-box newness. My previous birthday had produced the best present of my life, a BMX bike with extra tread on the tires. It was my transportation to and from school (since I hated the bus) and my favorite hobby. It was my most prized possession.

"You can leave it under the stairs."

"But ... ." I shocked myself that I spoke up. He tipped his head back and glared down at me through slits in his eyes. "But, someone will steal it," I managed.

"No one's going to steal it."

I heard my mother's voice in my head, "Eheeyah beseder." *It will be okay.*

Of course, it wasn't okay. Less than a week after we arrived, the bike was stolen. I was heartbroken and vowed to someday take revenge on the Greek mafia.

Alongside my imaginary scenarios, a real-life horror was playing out right in our neighborhood. In the fall of 1980, a twelve-year-old girl was abducted and murdered not far from our house. Over the next nine months, the notorious Clifford Olson abducted, raped, and murdered several young Vancouver girls, often writing letters to their parents describing every detail of his encounter with their daughter. Terrified parents put their kids on lockdown, with strict orders to stay inside while the police conducted one of the biggest manhunts in Canadian history.

I knew my orders, but by the summer of 1981, I thought I would go crazy if I didn't get outside. My father had just bought me a new foldable bike from England, and it was begging me to ride it. One July afternoon, I couldn't resist. Iris, on the phone upstairs, didn't see me slip my bike out the back door. I jumped on and raced to the park. It's a trip I'd made hundreds of times, and I felt wild and free as I ran across stumps and swung from the monkey bars. This time was different, however, because there wasn't another person in sight.

I may have been there fifteen minutes, or two hours, as my young brain never monitored time, when suddenly I felt my spine stiffen, as if an electric current was quietly invading my body. I slowly turned my head and saw an old brown VW van with no back windows idling in the parking lot. A lone man sat in the driver's seat, his eyes locked on mine. *Stranger.* My bike lay on the ground between us. I stared at it for a moment, as I tried to decide if I could beat him to it. I took one step forward, and his door opened. Adrenaline surged into my head. *Fight or flight?* My rehearsed scenarios sprang to life as I turned to flee.

Forget the bike. Move to where he cannot drive. You are smaller and faster. Just outrun him.

I jogged toward the trees in the middle of the park, hoping he would just get out for a smoke, and drive away. Perhaps my imagination was just in overdrive. But he didn't, and it wasn't. He slammed his door shut and peeled ahead, spraying rocks across the deserted parking lot. A small dirt road weaved through the trees, and he sped to cut me off.

I moved into another gear. I flew through the brush, limbs scratching my face and grabbing at my clothing, as the van sped parallel to me. The road bent in front of me, and soon we would intersect. I surged forward, my lungs and legs burning from the effort. I bound across the road just ahead of him, and scrambled through another patch of trees to the safety of the street.

I didn't slow down or look back. I thought my pounding heart would burst as I fell through the front door and stumbled into the kitchen. My mother and father sprang to their feet and started shouting and swearing over each other in several different languages. Apparently, I had been gone closer to two hours.

"Where in the hell have you been?" my father yelled, his hands alternating between waving erratically and smoothing down his hair. "Can't you follow directions? We've called the cops to look for you!"

"Leah, Leah, dear, what on earth were you thinking?" I could see the glistening in the corners of my mother's eyes. The gravity of what might have been started to sink in. My stomach tightened.

"I just went to the park for a while," I managed between heaving breaths, deciding not to further burden my already stressed parents. Besides, if I told them the truth, I might never get back to park. "It was fine, Mom. There were lots of kids there."

She eyed my scratched face and leaf-strewn hair suspiciously. "I just decided to run home, but I forgot my bike," I shrugged. My father walked back to the park and collected my bike, but not before giving me a sound spanking. Looking back, I can't imagine what thoughts flew through their minds that day.

Was the man in the brown van Clifford Olson? I have no idea. Two weeks later, after killing his eleventh victim, he was caught and Vancouver finally exhaled. But I'm not sure I ever did. I inhaled the feeling of helplessness, and couldn't let it go. I decided I was done fleeing. I needed to fight.

Arizona

"Call it a clan, call it a network, call it a tribe, call it a
family: Whatever you call it, whoever you are,
you need one."

Jane Howard

The descent into Death Valley has a nickname, "The Glass Elevator." The beautiful view almost distracts you from noticing the ever-increasing temperature. Almost. The road flattens out along the bottom, where you're forced to pedal against 110° wind and melting pavement that grabs at your sinking tires. I've raced in every condition imaginable, and know I must keep my wheels on the relatively cool white line.

My crew and parents continually leapfrog their vehicles around me, so they can spray me with cool water and switch my water bottles. The liquid is warm within twenty minutes no matter how much ice they add. I can feel my skin sizzling as I turn a sharp corner, and slow down enough to hear my father mumble, "You must have gotten dropped on your head."

He doesn't get it. There's no money to be made, it's dangerous as hell, and nobody's watching. But the truth is, I'm just like him.

Many people have theories on where my drive has come from. Did my parents expect greatness from me? Is my intense need to win in my DNA, inherited from my grandparents' survival skills? After all, my family tree has weaved its way through and survived concentration camps, communism, escapes, immigration, and a partridge in a pear tree. You name it; some close blood relative has probably faced it and somehow managed to thrive. Do I have some magical "winning gene," or have my parents pushed me to strive for seemingly impossible goals? It's so much more complicated than that.

My mother, Ahoova, grew up with her large family in Kulja (pronounced Koor-sha), now known as Yining, China. Her parents had emigrated from Russia in the 1920s, then married and started a family in the Northern Province of Xinjiang. The huge province, over 660,000 square miles (similar in size to Alaska) is surrounded by mountain ranges permanently covered in snow. The inhospitable Taklimakan Desert stretches across much of the interior, making the water basins along the borders the only habitable land. A true melting pot of cultures, Turkics, Muslim Uighurs, Han Chinese, Mongols, Russians, and many more lived alongside each other as China went through civil unrest and ultimately, conversion into Communism.

This rugged corner, at that time largely ignored by the growing pains of a new government, lived by old-world justice. "Клин клйном вышибáют," my grandfather Aaron would say. *Fight fire with fire.* Mountainous, dry terrain creates tough, sturdy people, and my people were among the toughest. By the early 1950s, Aaron and his wife Frieda had three houses, six kids, hundreds of dairy cows, and a wheel manufacturing business. They were comparatively wealthy, and often fed other families in the area. But wealth meant you had something to take, and Aaron protected his family and assets with vigilante justice.

The kids grew up speaking Chinese to the other kids and Russian at home. My mother, the eldest of six, thankfully learned a bit of the other dialects. Walking through the woods one day, my mother and her sister were approached by two Mongols on horseback.

"Look at these two pretty white girls. We could get a good price for them," the younger man said, smiling. Kidnappings were rare, but not unheard of.

"Our father is Aaron," yelled my mother in Mongolian. Calm and mature beyond her nine years, she set her chin at them, daring them to cross her father.

"What did she say?" said the older one.

"They are Aaron's. Let's go."

And with that, they wheeled their horses and ran off. My mother felt the safety of her father's reputation, while at the same time surviving his tirades at home. Aaron, an alcoholic his entire life, wouldn't stand for anyone laying a hand on his children, but thought nothing of backhanding or belting them himself. Ahoova became the protector, reading his moods and trying to keep the younger kids out of his way.

In the mid-1950s, Communism finally arrived in that remote corner of China, and practically overnight, the family lost everything. All the cattle, their houses, and the land were taken to be redistributed among the people. Many

Russians fled, including Aaron and Frieda. They packed their few remaining belongings into a wagon and drove their last horse to the nearby city of Ürümqi. Friends along the way had told them that many people were emigrating to Australia and Israel, but you had to get to their embassy in Shanghai—an impossible journey by horse and wagon.

The family checked into an overcrowded hotel to rest for a few nights. The owner of the hotel found out the family's plan to travel to Shanghai, and called the authorities. Everyone knew that defectors were traveling that way, and citizens were encouraged to "police" their neighbors. At midnight, the Communist police confronted the family and demanded that they return to Kulja immediately. My grandfather talked quickly and convinced them that they were just visiting relatives, and they were released. However, the officers gave him a stern warning that they had better not see him farther down the road. If the family were caught continuing toward Shanghai, the consequences would be disastrous—and my grandfather knew it.

Many families were trying to make their way out of China at this time. Shanghai, home to the Israeli and Australian embassies, was the portal to freedom. Once registered as a potential immigrant, China would allow families to leave. Aaron and Frieda weren't even sure which country they would end up in, but knew they must at least get to Shanghai. The next afternoon he took a nap. During the nap, Aaron had a dream about how they were going to get there.

In the dream, he walked to the airport and got tickets.

Then he shaved his face, cut his hair to look more Asian, and bought Chinese clothes for himself and his wife. As soon as he woke up, that's exactly what he did. He cut his hair, shaved, redressed, and walked straight to the airport. He miraculously found a Russian pilot willing to transport illegal passengers and paid him with the few valuables they had left. The next night, Aaron and Frieda loaded their children and bags into two rickshaws and headed to the airport.

They covered all the kids with blankets to make them look like baggage. It was a stormy night, and soon after getting to the airport, the pilot informed them that the plane could not take off. The pilot let them spend the night there, the kids sleeping on cots. Aaron and Frieda were terrified; they paced all night, fearing the rickshaw drivers would alert the authorities. They didn't, and the next morning the family flew safely to Shanghai—the first leg of their journey was successful. They were hopeful, but broke. And as soon as the government knew that the family had applied for visas, no one was allowed to even get a job.

They found a small apartment near the harbor, where most immigrants lived and Aaron started sharpening knives to earn enough money for rent. The kids adjusted from being rich and envied to scrounging for food and being openly mocked on the streets. White people were the Shanghai minority, and most of them were in the process of leaving the country. The Chinese people knew it, and didn't hesitate to call them "dirty immigrants" and worse.

In Communist China, all food and goods were rationed. The ration lines for rice, oil, and other staples started filling up around four o'clock in the morning, so to be assured of food for the day, they would have to be in line by then. And *all* of them would have to go—one ticket, one person, and one ration. Aaron would carry the little ones, who were too tired to stand in line.

The family wasn't particularly religious in Kulja, but in Shanghai, grandfather dragged them all to the synagogue every day. I'm sure it improved their immigration chances if they proved they were devout, and grandfather wasn't taking any chances. The kids loathed going, but at least they created a network of friends and supporters while they waited four long years to be approved by Israel.

They had help along the way. A man even paid for my Aunt Udit's meningitis treatments—three months in the hospital and two injections per day for months after. Another relief-aid worker from England gave the children extra food. My mother assures me that, without this help, they might have starved like so many others.

At last, the family got approval and took the month-long boat trip to Israel. Grandfather somehow purchased some land in Beit Hillel in northern Israel, and the family moved back to a farm. They grew watermelon, pumpkin, and corn, and raised dairy cows. My mother and her brothers and sisters worked very hard to improve the Hebrew they'd started to learn in Shanghai. Luckily, their first teacher was from Russia and was sympathetic to the new kids.

My mother quickly became the sentry to all the little kids in the area, including her own five siblings. One day, a boy her age asked if they wanted to go swimming with some of his friends. She agreed and started herding everyone down toward the river. The boy asked her, "So, you can swim, right?"

My mother was offended and quickly replied, "Of course, I can swim!" Except, she actually couldn't swim. She had never gone swimming in her life. She was petrified, but had too much pride to admit that she'd lied. She jumped straight in to the deep water of the Jordan River, and immediately began to drown. She slid down under the water, until only the end of her long, thick braid clung to the top of the water. The boy, swimming nearby, got scared and pulled her back up to the surface.

"What's wrong with you? Swim!" he yelled.

And she did. Her twenty-second swimming lesson complete, she paddled back to shore to jump in again. I can just hear the voice in her head: *Drowning? Not that bad. Admitting I can't do something? Never. Just jump!* She is wild and hardheaded like me. Neither of us ever likes being told we can't do something.

She begged her parents to let her play sports. They never approved, so of course she went right out and signed up for the track team. She was so talented that she'd often compete in five or six events. In one particular meet, she landed awkwardly on her last long jump. She won, but needed help to get out of the sand pit. A few girls ran over, panicked—she was still needed for the final race. She assured everyone that she was okay, and still anchored a victory for the relay team. The next day, she took a bus to the hospital where they put a full-length cast on her broken leg.

Her childhood had offered a lifetime of fears and discomforts, and by the time she was a teenager, excuses just never occurred to her. She always seemed unflinchingly brave to me, just like Bruce Lee or the many fictional secret agents I had created in my head. My mother never used phrases like "Maybe you shouldn't." or "Are you sure?" No matter what I asked or proposed to do with my life, she has always replied, "Of course you can."

I glanced to my left, and could see pigs running alongside me in the opposite ditch. I decided they weren't real, and turned my head back to the road. A moment later, the follow-car pulled up beside me honking the horn, Janessa leaning out the window yelling and waving her arms. The pigs were real, and had turned across the road making a beeline straight for my bike. Sean gunned the engine and cut them off.

"You okay, Leah?" Janessa asked through the open window, half laughing.

"Were those wild pigs?" I yelled over the engine.

"Yeah! Who knew they were so aggressive?"

"Seriously. And I'm Jewish for God's sake! I don't even eat pork!"

Around the next corner, my parents stood beside my dad's white pick-up. My mother's eyes met mine and she nodded and half smiled, trying to hide the concern in her eyes. This race was different than any in my past, riding in the dark, fighting sleep, and trusting the thousands of motorists en route to give me a wide berth. This one was more stressful for her, I could tell.

"Some pigs just tried to run me off the road!" I yelled, trying to make her laugh.

"Oh, good. Let's catch one and we'll cook you some bacon!" she yelled back. My father's not the only one with snappy comebacks, especially when it comes to pork. Pig jokes are twice as funny to us.

My father's father was named, Dov, which means "Bear" in Hebrew, but standing barely five feet tall, his family joked that he was more like a mouse. He survived several brushes with death during World War II, possibly because he was brave. Maybe he was just lucky. Certainly, he survived at least one brush with death because he was small.

In the spring of 1940, Germany began clearing out the Jewish Ghetto in Warsaw where my grandfather's family had been barely surviving. After several years of inhumane living conditions and despair, the Nazis were simply "cleaning house," taking some people as workers and shooting the rest. News of the concentration camps and mass genocide hadn't reached most of the Western world yet, at least not enough to actually be believed. But most Polish Jews knew exactly what was happening to their friends and family, locked into trains and cargo trucks, never to be seen again. The illusion of work camps and temporary housing had long been abandoned.

Dov, his six brothers, two of his four sisters, plus a handful of their friends had spent several days hiding in the top floor of an abandoned building. They could glimpse out of the top floor window and see the tanks and troops closing in on Warsaw, but there was no escape, nowhere left to run. The fear and desperation quietly enveloped the little group as the sounds of tank treads gave way to German voices, yelling orders to search their building. The group knew they only had a few minutes at most to make their last free decision, one moment to consider their bleak options.

A few searched desperately for a place to hide, including my grandfather. An overweight Jew at that time was unheard of—everyone was perpetually hungry. But my grandfather was an extra-scrawny teenager, and managed to wedge his body between the inner and outer wall of the room. Dov practically stopped breathing as he strained to hear. The soldiers' boots on the stairway grew louder amidst the whispered prayers and goodbyes of his brothers and friends. He braced himself for gunshots, but all he heard was the sound of shoes scraping against the window frame, as one by one, every person jumped to their death.

The soldiers assumed everyone had jumped and simply moved to the next building. Dov waited until the tank sounds faded, and then made a break for the border. He escaped into Russia and joined the Red Army. After the fall of the Nazis, he returned to Poland only to discover that of his parents and ten siblings, he was the only survivor.

He married my grandmother, Devora, who had survived two years in Auschwitz. They moved to Poland and had three sons. My father remembers the neighborhood, full of hungry kids whose fathers would take their government or meager paychecks straight to the bar, trying to drink away their memories. Dov, a shoemaker, made enough money to keep food on the table for his family and often for other kids needing a meal.

Although they tried to return to "normal" life, remnants of the war continued to plague them. My father's youngest brother, Matie, was just a toddler when he opened an old cupboard in their basement, setting off a bomb that cost him his eye. A few months later, two German men forced their way into their home in the middle of the night. They opened two secret compartments built into the stone fireplace and took everything inside, obviously reclaiming stashed goods from the occupation.

Dov and Devora decided to start over in Israel.

But the war followed them. They raised their kids, but the flashbacks and trauma had created cold, distant parents. The three boys grew up quickly, often living in a kibbutz, a self-sustaining community with gardens, often a restaurant, and rooms for rent. Everyone living on the property gets free room and board, in exchange for working in the kitchen, on the grounds, in maintenance or hospitality. The kibbutz provided a safe, comfortable place for the boys to finish school.

My father Sam loathed his mandatory military service (all men serve three years; women serve two) and snuck out of the base several times. He had met my mother just before he reported for duty, and, after watching her fearlessly jump from a 10-meter swimming pool platform, decided she would be his wife. He'd occasionally slip under the fence to visit her in nursing school, fearful that she'd meet someone else during his absence. He got caught once, and stood before the disciplinary officer.

"Leaving the base is a serious offense, soldier. Why did you do it?" he asked.

"I had to work. My mother and younger brothers need extra money." That time, it was actually true.

The commander looked over his file and shook his head.

"You're a good soldier." My father felt relieved. Perhaps he'd just get a warning. "But you'll be an even better soldier after thirty days in prison."

My father served his sentence at the notorious Prison #6, rumored to house the worst military offenders. The guard walked him in and sat him in a barber chair. The barber held clippers in his hand and joked, "How would you like it." My father, never without a witty comeback replied, "Just make me look like Elvis." He walked out nearly bald, the mandatory hairstyle of prisoners.

The cells held four men, each with a cot and blanket. After breakfast each day, the beds were removed and the cell filled with shin-deep water. For the rest of the day, no one could even sit—unless one was willing to soak his body in putrid water. Men were occasionally allowed to leave for work projects in exchange for cigarettes; my father always volunteered. He'd smoke some of the cigarettes, but he always saved a few to use as bribes for his cellmates. In exchange for a cigarette, his roommates were willing to spend thirty minutes on their hands and knees in the stale water and let my father sit on their backs. He never finished high school, but the guy was a born entrepreneur.

My parents planned to marry after my father finished a year with the Merchant Marines, when he sailed all over the world. His brief visit to Vancouver stuck in his mind, and he convinced my mother that they could make a lot of money there. My mother didn't want to leave her family, so they agreed to just live in Canada until they had saved up $10,000, and then they would move back. We all joke that they're still waiting to make that ten grand.

They stayed, yet, interestingly, I always felt that I belonged in Israel rather than Canada. During our yearly visits, I'd stay with my grandparents, Aaron and Frieda near the Jordan River and work the farm with them. I'd run with their twenty dogs through the pecan tree grove and ride in their horse-drawn cart. My grandfather would catch me a wild rabbit as a pet, or give me a calf, and I'd want to stay to take care of them.

The Israeli security forces also fascinated me, and even as a young child, I knew that someday I would enlist in the army and work my way up to the famed international secret service, the Mossad. Military service is mandatory in Israel, so the entire population are ex-soldiers. I'd listen, fascinated, as my uncles, cousins, and family friends spoke about their time in the army. I was born in Canada and, therefore, had no legal obligation to Israel, but I didn't give that a second thought. I knew my life plan required that I join. Someday.

I felt so connected to Israel that I'd often cry and ask my parents to stay longer. But one thing always drew me back to Vancouver—my ninth birthday and tae kwon do.

The road seemed to wobble as my headlight swayed hypnotically in tempo with my pedaling legs. *I actually feel tired now.* I pressed my radio button.

"Hey—are we planning to stop soon?" I asked Ed and Lori, following right behind me.

"Yeah, only about fifteen more minutes and we have a motel room ready for you," Lori replied. "Are you actually going to sleep this time?" she mocked.

I nodded. We had stopped the previous night, and

after I'd showered and eaten a bit, they'd left me to sleep for a couple hours. I tried to, but the people in the room next to me were not trying, if you catch my drift. I kept thinking, if I just waited five more minutes, it would be over and I could nod off. I waited those five minutes, about five times. Then I gave up, got dressed, and knocked on the crew's room door.

"Let's go—I can't sleep."

We carried on for another twenty-four hours before I started to feel drowsy again. Thankfully, they had picked a perfect stopping point, and that night I slept for ninety minutes. And then they knocked on my door.

"No more sleeping! Let's go!"

From the first time I stepped into Choi's Martial Arts School, that building was my church. I went for lessons twice a week and occasionally on Saturdays—often waiting at the door for my instructor to arrive. I never missed training. Sick, hurt, family plans—everything had to be put aside for my class. Choi was impressed with me right away—I had been doing my own style of training mimicking Bruce for years, and I was a very eager student.

My first group was about twenty people, mostly men. Tae kwon do attracted very few kids at that time and even fewer women. I was shy and quiet, so I just kept my head down and tried to outwork everyone in the room. I started going to tournaments shortly thereafter, and quickly learned the art of moving up the tae kwon do chain. Each belt requires a series of movements, called forms. A competitor has to master these forms before moving up a belt color, starting at white and advancing through yellow, green, blue, red and finally, to black. At a tournament, I would compete in forms in the morning and then spar against other same-colored belts in the evening. In the Junior Division, boys and girls competed against each other, no matter what size they were. I was thin and small, but I never felt outmatched by anyone. Within two years, I was a red belt and had never lost a fight. I was pretty good at forms too, but I really liked the chess game of actual hand-to-hand combat.

When I was twelve, Choi took a group of us to the North American Championships in Portland, Oregon. I had just gotten a black stripe added to my red belt, so I was just one step from being a black belt. It didn't really matter though, since red and black belts fight each other anyway. We all fought round-robin matches in the morning, and then were seeded into a single elimination tournament for the afternoon. The two junior hotshots, both Americans and both black belts, finished the morning undefeated, as did I. One kid was a giant, one of those twelve-year-old boys who look like they could probably be shaving already. He stood almost a head taller than me and was twice as thick.

But he wasn't the fighter I couldn't take my eyes off, the one favored to win it all.

The top ranked American was a smaller Chinese boy and, in my young mind, this meant that he possessed some ingrained, ancient knowledge of martial arts that a white Canadian girl could never grasp. His shiny black hair hung in a perfect bowl around his unsmiling Bruce Lee face. His kicks flew impossibly high, and his fists whirled in a blur as he demolished opponent after opponent. In between matches, his Chinese coaches would huddle together with him, demonstrating blocks and punches in their superior Chinese way. I looked around for Choi. He walked between his fifteen students, all of different ages and categories, and offered nods and pats on the back. He didn't have time for more. I watched mini Bruce Lee with his support crew and for the first time realized that I didn't have a coach. I had a teacher. I checked the elimination chart. If I kept winning, I would meet him in the semifinal.

We both easily advanced, as did man-boy in the other bracket. He'd won his semifinal and stood alongside the many other spectators to see if he'd fight mini-Bruce or the skinny, white girl from Vancouver.

The announcer called my Chinese opponent's name, and a loud cheer went up. Choi stood beside me, knowing what I was thinking. "You are faster," he clipped, and gave my shoulder a gentle shove forward. I walked onto the mat amidst yells and claps from the other Choi fighters, took a deep breath, and turned to face him.

I waited and watched, as he danced and kicked, his movements graceful and beautiful. They were also totally predictable. He took the first two points, as I was still taking mental notes on his patterns. Our matches, only two rounds of sixty seconds, didn't offer much waiting time. So after thirty seconds of watching, I started fighting. I slowed his movements down in my mind, and could see his leg kicking before it had left the ground. I easily ducked and landed two solid punches. His fists flew at me, but in my mind they seemed robotic and obvious, as I blocked them faster than he could throw them.

I could feel his frustration build, as his control and grace faded. Mini-Bruce was the best fighter I'd ever faced, and the challenge required a shift, a deeper concentration than I'd ever had before. My mind and body responded, and I peppered him with kicks and fists. The final bell rang and we bowed toward one another. It's a sign of respect, and although I'd bowed to numerous opponents in the past, this was the first one I felt. I kept my face calm and stoic, while the adults from Vancouver all shook my shoulders and smiled in my face. I pretended as though I knew I would win all along, and kept my chin a little higher than normal all the way back to the locker room. I knew man-boy was watching me, and instinctively I wanted him to fear me.

He probably had watched the Chinese contingent all afternoon as I had, never suspecting he'd actually be fighting me for the title. And after watching the semifinal, he was afraid. I could feel it. And as I stepped onto the mat to face him, I thought, "You should be." I felt invincible as I blocked his meaty hands and lumbering kicks, partly because I was flying on adrenaline and partly because he gave me too much respect. He fought on his heels, unsure and hesitant. I took advantage and easily defeated him. After that bell rang, I allowed my head to drop and let reality sink in. I'd beaten them both. I looked over at a smiling Choi, who raised his eyebrows and gave me three quick nods, as if to say, "See? I said you were faster."

"Leah. Leah!"

I lurch my head up, the faded white line barely visible in the soft glow of my bike light.

"Keep your head up! Only five more kilometers, and then we'll stop for a rest." It's Connie on the radio. *Thank God. I need to get off for a minute.*

"Leah!" I jerk my head up again. *Am I falling asleep?*

"You're falling asleep! Take some deep breaths. Do you want me to start singing to you?"

I hear Rob the paramedic laughing in the background. *At least they are awake.* I manage to press my response button.

"If I promise to keep my head up, will you promise not to sing?" More laughter.

I can just make out the outline of a gnarly stump in the ditch, which quickly grows arms and its root-like hands begin clawing at the dirt. I know it's a hallucination, but I can still feel my bike sway a few inches into the road. I've only slept for two hours out of the past forty, and am actually surprised the imaginary friends have held off this long. Sleep-deprived brains have a tendency to hallucinate. Add physical exertion and, for me at least, they become intense, vivid, and often scary. It's like being in a dream that you know is a dream, but you still can't help running from the monster or staring in awe at the brightly colored clouds or little dancing elves. It's not real. But it's still entertaining.

UTAH

"I love to see a young girl go out and grab the world by the lapels. Life's a bitch. You've got to go out and kick ass."

Maya Angelou

Lori held my arm as I wobbled into a gas station restroom.

"Why are you walking like that?" she asked.

I saw dead kittens on the floor. They were everywhere, all different colors and sizes, and I didn't want to step on them.

"There are cats," I mumbled, as I carefully tiptoed through the bodies.

"Hmmm, okay." My crew was getting used to my "visions."

I wasn't upset or shocked by the sight; therefore, on some level I knew they weren't real. But I still couldn't step on them.

While in the bathroom, I changed my shorts, brushed my teeth, and listened through the door as Lori tried to explain our situation to the gas station attendant.

"She's in what kind of a bike race?"

"It's called ultra-distance. This race goes from California to Maryland."

"Well, I've just never heard of anything like that! She has to ride it all by herself?"

"We follow her in a van, but basically, yeah, she does."

"Oh, the poor thing! She looks so tired and worn out!"

"Very. But she signed up for it."

No mercy.

It's a delicate balance, crewing for a RAAM racer. I want them to care about me, of course. Safety is paramount, and when my brain turns mushy, I need them to make decisions for me. Taking sleep breaks, eating, and drinking, and even when to change my shorts are decided by the crew. But I also need them to keep me racing. As races get longer, the breaks feel better and better, and can really eat up your time. I warned them at the starting line that I wanted to race this, not ride it. So they had to be taskmasters when it came to time off the bike.

"Let's go, Princess!" Lori pounded on the door.

Several of the crew used that little nickname, as my name is pronounced the same as the famous Princess Leia from *Star Wars*. I cringed. I'd never seen the movies, but was pretty sure I didn't fit the comparison. It felt good to stand in the bathroom though, so I ignored her and took one last look around the floor. *Goodbye little cats. Don't worry—you aren't actually dead.*

I loved martial arts, but after the Portland tournament I started feeling restless and looking at other disciplines. I had switched to the women's tae kwon do division, and the competition felt like a joke. I easily won matches but often got yellow cards for excessive force. Tae kwon do matches require control and precision, but not full contact. I just couldn't seem to contain myself.

My father was a good boxer in his day and had a heavy bag in the garage. He'd started showing me how to stand, move, and punch like a boxer. I liked the idea of throwing my weight into an attack, crushing my fist into the bag. During a break one day at Choi's, I was dancing around a dummy, slamming my fists into his gut and head, ducking and weaving the imaginary counterattacks. A Chinese guy named John, a fellow black belt, stood and watched me, grinning.

"Hey, ya know what, Leah? Maybe you should try kick-boxing?" he said.

He may have been kidding, sarcastically pointing out that I shouldn't be fighting like that. But I took it as an opening. An adult fighter thought I'd make a good kickboxer. That was enough for me.

There was a tiny studio on Kingsway that advertised "Praying Mantis—Kung Fu" and in small letters underneath, "Kickboxing." I rode my bike down there one day, and with my head held high, I walked in. Looking back, I'm actually surprised my head even fit through the doorway. Not that the entry was that small (although almost everything else in that studio was), but my head was that big.

I was really good at tae kwon do—great even. It just came easily to me. My coach would often show me off to potential new clients—pairing me with a grown man and letting us spar. It was almost as if to say, "Look at how effective my teaching style is—this twelve-year-old can beat a man!" And I could. Pound for pound, I would've bet on me against anyone. I waltzed all one hundred pounds of myself into Alen Chang's studio, ready to train like a kickboxer.

The atmosphere was completely opposite of Choi's. At the tae kwon do studio, everyone wore matching white dobok (uniforms), the floor was clean, and the mirrors pristine. It was extremely organized and strict. Talking or goofing around was not tolerated, and our precise training exercises were performed on gleaming mats.

Chang's studio was tiny—a closet really. The floor looked like it was a hundred years old and there was one cracked mirror on the wall. Eight young men were busy training in the cramped space. It appeared they had just thrown on whatever dirty clothes they could find that morning, including the socks. The smell was overpowering. I had never been in a boxing gym, and nothing quite prepares you for the reek created by stale sweat pouring out of a boxing glove. Chang's studio was small, smelly, and didn't even have a ring. It was just a raw, boxing sweatfest—and I fell in love.

Alen Chang came right over to me and introduced himself. He was barely taller than me, and not much heavier.

"I Alen Chang—and who you?" he said, in his barely understandable English.

"I'm Leah Goldstein," I replied, relishing the slight raise of his eyebrows. I thought for sure he had heard of me.

"Oh, yeah? What can I do for you?"

"I want to try kickboxing."

"Really?" His eyes were sparkling. From excitement or amusement, I couldn't tell.

"You come tomorrow, 4 o'clock. We give you try," he stated as he turned back to his ragtag group of boxers.

I practically floated out of there from excitement. I was a second-degree black belt—an actual licensed dangerous weapon. I could hardly wait until the next day so I could show them all how tough I was.

Life lessons present themselves in harsh ways sometimes, and the first day of kickboxing was the first of many
tough lessons to come. Alen told me to warm up, and then
I would do some sparring. I did a little jump rope and
stretching. *Don't go too hard on this kid; he probably doesn't
have as much experience as me. Just play with him a bit and
show Alen my skills.* Eagerly, I shoved my hands into the
padded boxing gloves. Alen pulled the laces tight and tied
neat tiny bows on each wrist. I waited for a comment—but
he just pounded my hands together and shoved a mouth
guard against my upper teeth.

Gavin, as I later learned his name to be, stood casually
across from me. "Okay, let's go," blurted Alen, and I went
straight at him. I danced and punched and threw my best
high kicks. And for the first minute or so, I convinced myself that although I hadn't really connected a good punch,
he was definitely on the defensive and it was only a matter
of time. But as the seconds ticked by, I could hear my heavy
breathing and feel my arms getting heavier—a sure sign
of fatigue. That's when he attacked. Wham! His right foot
slammed into the side of my thigh. My knee buckled and
tears sprang to my eyes. I barely had time to blink them
back when his left foot followed suit. I had never been
kicked like that in my life—my thighs screamed in pain
and I lost all control of my legs. I just couldn't kick him
back.

That's when he switched to his hands. Bam! My head
spun to the right. Bam! My head shot up and pulled my
body backwards. Punches came out of nowhere—to my

stomach, my nose, my chin, and both sides of my head. I couldn't believe it. I was a black belt! I was undefeated for my entire tae kwon do career; yet here I was fighting an amateur in red sweatpants and a cut-off t-shirt, and I couldn't even defend myself. Each punch created more anger in me, and I tried even harder. And that just led to him punching me even more. He kicked the crap out of me.

Thankfully, Alen stopped us. Gavin tapped my gloves, smiled, and said, "Nice fight."

I was practically hyperventilating, panting like a dog. Alen told me to calm down as he peeled off my gloves. I was embarrassed for sure, but even more pissed off. I'd spent four years training almost non-stop, assuming that my black belt meant something. It meant that I was tough; that I could protect myself from all the bad people (that I was sure were out there). But I couldn't. What a waste of time. *There's no way Alen will want to train me now.*

"Kickboxing is different sport. You good at tae kwon do, but dat is not fighting. Kickboxer is fighter."

I couldn't even look at him. I stared into the dirty, cracked mirror and watched blood drip over my lips. My eyes were starting to swell and my whole face was bright pink.

"You better go home now."

I grabbed my gym bag, avoided eye contact with the rest of the boxers, and jumped on my bike. My head was pounding and my legs were killing me, but I rode as hard as I ever had, pushing faster and faster up the hills to my house. I threw my bike in the backyard and ran up the steps, still trying to catch my breath. I slammed the back door behind me and my mother came out of the kitchen.

"What happened?" she yelled. "Who did this to you?" She assumed I'd been mugged.

I turned and looked into the hallway mirror. My eye was nearly swollen shut and blood continued to trickle from my mouth down my neck. We both stared at my mangled face, her eyes incredulous and searching, waiting for an answer. My face steeled, already prepared for what was to come.

"I'm going to be a kickboxer, Mom."

She sighed, knowing it was useless to protest. "Okay, I'll get you some ice."

The next day, I entered Chang's studio with my eyes down, sliding along the wall to find an open spot for my bag. I could feel the eyes staring at me, just as I knew they would, and even though I truly hated being the center of attention, I was compelled to go back. The reeking studio already felt like home, as if we were magnets destined to slam together.

Alen walked over, seemingly unsurprised that I had returned.

"In three years, you be a World Champion," he stated, quietly and honestly.

And I, standing there with a fat lip and black eyes, believed him.

We got to work right away, mapping out a plan for training.

"You run 10 kilometers before school. At lunch, hit heavy bag. And night, you come here. You in bed by 8:00 p.m. and you eat only good food. You no time friends."

I wasted no time questioning anything Chang said. From the beginning, his word was gospel, and I just obeyed. My mind swirled with times, charts, calendars, and food tracking. It was almost a relief, this all-consuming sport. I could focus on fitness instead of school, and fighting instead of friendships. My face must have revealed my inner joy.

"And no smiling. Ever."

"Okay," I said. *No problem.*

Chang believed that the energy I gave off could defeat an opponent before we even exchanged blows. Smiling showed weakness. Plus, he didn't want me to get wrinkles, and he was convinced that smiling caused them. I hardly cracked a grin for the next three years.

I went home and started taking notes.

Shower: 4 minutes

Getting dressed: 1 minute

Getting dressed in rainy weather: 2 minutes

Eating: 6 minutes

Bathroom: 1 minute

And on the list went. I timed everything. How long it took to walk to school, ride my bike to school, take the bus to the studio, run home from the studio. Everything. I started a lifelong study of time, never wasting a second on TV or friends—unless it was in the schedule.

We started training with two months of Praying Mantis, a form of Kung Fu, known for its grace and control.

"Boxing should be beautiful, no messy!" Chang insisted. He cringed explaining the women's boxing he'd seen. "All cat fight. So messy. You not do dis!"

The martial arts training was meant to create control and restraint in my fighting, but the fluid, elegant movements didn't come naturally to me. Tae kwon do forms had required power and precision, but no grace. Going through the slow, methodical Praying Mantis skills felt awkward and forced. I just wanted to fight.

"Kung Fu, mean 'great sacrifice lead to great skill.' You must give up things, so you can succeed. You understand?"

I nodded, not smiling. Praying Mantis requires great inner strength, learning to smoothly "load" your body and then unleash that power into your hands, arms, and legs. We shifted to kickboxing training soon after, but Chang always incorporated Kung Fu into our training, using nunchucks and swords. Nunchucks are ancient weapons comprising two sets of two short sticks connected by chain or wire. One end is held in the user's hands, and the second stick whips around in various patterns. Used correctly, even a lightweight set could kill a person. I liked the nunchuck and sword work, but couldn't understand why we'd waste so much time away from boxing training. Over time, I would learn his secondary motive—Kung Fu movies.

Chang was from Hong Kong, and he predicted those studios would soon be making martial arts movies with non-traditional heroes, like small white girls. Thinking of my future, he'd say, "You no box forever. You movie star."

I didn't have the heart to tell him that my future was already planned. I had known my life path since I was four years old: join the Israeli military and become a Mossad agent. I'd tell him someday, but first, I had to box.

I was just fourteen years old when Alen booked me in my first fight. A local Wang Chung club offered to take on any challengers in an exhibition event, and he decided I was ready. In training, Chang sparred with me in the Wang Chung style with a wide stance and long open arms. He rolled his eyes at the style, telling me that if I attacked quickly and fiercely, I shouldn't have a problem winning the fight.

"Just don't get hit, okay?"

I nodded.

Wang Chung style leaves the fighter vulnerable, as their arms are spread wide apart. They throw mostly huge swinging punches, spinning their body around like a sprinkler. Their advantage, then, was if they did make good contact with their opponent, they would probably knock them out.

Warming up before the fight, I kept glancing over at my opponent. At twenty-eight, she had years of experience and close to 15 pounds on me. The event was a non-World Karate Association event, and, therefore, had no weigh in. Anyone could fight anyone else. But her size didn't scare me. She was Chinese. That's what scared me. Again, the stereotype haunted me.

She looks just like Bruce Lee's sister. Oh my gosh, I'm going to get killed.

Chang pulled my head around to his.

"You look here. No matter about her. Focus only here."

When we finally ducked into the ring, I felt like I might pass out from nerves. Chang grabbed my gloves.

"You beat her. Remember you practice dis. Stay on inside,

close to her. She want distance to throw her big punch, but you no let her. You beat her."

The bell rang, and all my nervous energy gathered in my torso. I hopped from foot to foot, feeling the electricity fill my arms and legs. She slowly circled me, and threw a few big swings. I avoided them easily, and felt my confidence grow. I darted in for a quick combo. I hit her temple and nose, and shocked myself at how powerful the blows felt. She came at me with renewed vigor, wildly swinging her right arm. I saw an opening, threw in my right hand, and then felt the satisfying *crack* as I landed a solid punch to her nose. Her eyes widened, as did mine. Suddenly, bright red blood gushed down her face. She turned back to her corner as her trainers jumped in the ring with towels and ice.

The four-round fight was over in less than two minutes. Her crew called the fight and the referee pulled my hand into the air. Winner by technical knockout (TKO). I still didn't smile as the guys from Chang's studio whistled and yelled for me. They all had come to watch, even though only three of us fought that day. I could hear my heart racing, not from the effort but from something else entirely. During the fight, I had felt a click inside me, as if a piece of my soul had finally slid into place. I belonged here.

At last, I was in the right place. I was a kickboxer, and not in the sense that it was something I did, but it was who I was. I looked over at Chang and wondered if he was thinking the same thing as me.

No woman will ever beat me in a ring. I own this sport.

Within a year, I'd knocked out my next two opponents, both heavier and older than me. Women's kickboxing, while moderately popular, didn't really have enough serious fighters in each category, so promoters often mixed the weight classes. Plus the crowds, full of Hell's Angels and small-time gamblers, wanted to see a mismatch. They wanted to see someone get crushed. And at barely fifteen-years-old, and 115 pounds, that someone was supposed to be me.

But I never felt outmatched by anyone. In fact, in my first few fights, I was barely touched. And by the end of that third fight, a sanctioned event in Coquitlam where I knocked my opponent out in the second round, I could feel the crowd's support shift to me.

As easy as the fights were, training was sweet torture. I loved the physical work, always running farther and punching harder than I was told, but I started to feel effects from the repetitive head contact. I always sparred with the guys, and often came home with fat lips and black eyes. My nose bled so badly once I had to get it cauterized. I often saw stars, and felt dizzy after a sparring match. Chang never took it easy on me though, pushing me to attack faster and recover more quickly.

He'd blindfold me and punch my face at half-speed, while I learned to move away from the force. He wanted my reaction to be automatic; no thought. At the end of each session, he treated my shins to a fast, repetitive drumming session with bamboo sticks. The slapping numbed the nerve endings, allowing my lower legs to block and kick without hesitation from pain.

Alen then mapped out my next two years: B.C. Championship, National Championship, and then World Championship. After that, I'd retire. We never discussed what we would do if I lost. The thought never crossed our minds.

Leading up to the Provincial Championship bout, I trained even harder. A few of my father's friends had been professional boxers back in Poland, and they met me occasionally in our converted garage. I bought books on boxing training and grilled them with questions about skipping rope workouts, interval runs (alternating sprinting and jogging), punching techniques, and even weight control.

Bantamweights fight at 118 pounds, and I became obsessed with how much I weighed. Stepping on the scale became part of my over-planned day.

Weigh-In Pre-Workout: 30 Seconds

Weigh-In Post-Workout: 30 Seconds

My diet leaned down to fish, eggs, vegetables, fruit, and a rare, tiny slice of my mother's honey cake. I never ate sugar, bread, pasta, junk food, or fast food. I felt that I couldn't waste a calorie; everything was measured and written down. But I still felt strong. Thin and fierce. Chang thought thinner was better too, reminding me that a light body is easier to move fast. He insisted that I always wear long sleeves, though, so my opponents wouldn't see just how skinny I was.

The Provincial Championship fights were held in 100 Mile House, which is the exact middle-of-nowhere British Columbia. The community center, however, was packed with tattoos, leather jackets, and flannel shirts, everyone chanting for the show. I couldn't believe this many people would come to a kickboxing match. The card listed all male fights, except for mine. And I don't know what it was about women's fights at that time, but it always brought the crowd to its feet. Our fight was saved for last—the main event.

The early fights took longer than normal. I paced and watched, trying to stave off my nerves. Another hour passed, and I realized my bout wouldn't start until well after dinnertime. My stomach growled. I walked over to the snack bar, and looked at all the chocolate bars. Not a vegetable in sight. *I'm not going to make it through the fight. I have to eat something!* I saw Alen come into the gym, and I quickly slid away. I didn't want anyone to see me even looking at junk food.

I went back into the warm-up area, and took thirty cents out of my bag. I snuck back to the snack bar, and waited until all eyes were on the ring. I threw the money on the counter, and grabbed the closest bar, a peanut butter Wunderbar. I sprinted down to the bathroom and locked myself in a stall, terrified to be seen. I chastised myself for not bringing my own, healthy snacks, but the Wunderbar was so delicious I enjoyed every peanut-butter-and-chocolate bite. I knew I would burn it off in the fight.

I rinsed out my mouth and checked my teeth in the mirror, then ran out to find Alen. He was just pulling out my jump rope.

"Where were you? It's time to start."

"Just staying loose in the hallway," I said, grabbing the rope. *Hope he can't smell my breath.*

"Kick her ass, Goldstein!" they shouted. "No mercy! Kill her!"

Whistles and shouts filled the auditorium. A few fans tried to high-five me as I jogged in, and I actually thought I recognized a few men from the tough-looking crowd. *I think that guy is from Vancouver! They would come all the way up here to watch me?*

The reigning champ fought clean and tough in the first round, but she was no match for my speed and they had to stop the fight for yet another bloody nose. In the second round, I landed a crushing front kick to her stomach and she fell to one knee. The ref completed the standing eight-count, and called the fight. Another TKO. I'd been a kickboxer for almost two years, and had fought in the ring for a total of about seven minutes.

"How much longer is this climb?" I radioed the van that had just disappeared around a corner. During the day, I liked the crew to stay parked on the road's shoulder as I rode past. They'd stand outside sometimes and offer fresh drinks or food. If I wanted it, I'd throw my old bottle or wrapper on the ground, and grab the fresh stuff from their outstretched arm. The crew would pick up my cast-offs and wait until I'd ridden ahead about a half-mile. Then the van would again pull ahead of me, park on the shoulder, and do it all over again.

"About one more mile, and then it's pretty flat for twenty. You okay?" asked Sean, referring to my choice of bike.

"Yeah, I'll make it."

It's a delicate dance, switching from road bike to time trial (TT) bike throughout 3,000 miles of roads. At the time, I was riding my TT bike, and the compact frame makes climbing difficult. My knees bumped the handlebars when I stood up. But for the time I'd waste switching bikes, it wouldn't be worth it. *What's a couple of bruised knees?*

I started to wonder if I would ever face a challenging opponent, and Chang assured me that the reigning Canadian Champion, Dale Bakey, would finally give me a good fight. Her husband, also named Dale, was her manager and a Vancouver promoter. He arranged a title match at the run-down Royal Towers Hotel in a nearby suburb. The press had started hearing about me, the teenager knocking out opponents, and they spread the word that this could be a fight to watch.

Dale definitely had much more experience, and Chang didn't take this fight lightly. We studied tapes of her past bouts, estimating which moves she favored and when she'd make them. He'd mimic her fighting style in the ring and talk me through visualization techniques.

"You must see each combination and counterattack before you make move," he coached. "You watch these in your head every day. Every day."

I lay in bed each night and pictured twenty different scenarios, and repeated them over and over until I fell asleep. *Attack right thigh, block left shin, jab, hook. Attack left head, duck, flying kick. Again!*

I repeated the combinations warming up on fight night, shadow boxing with a mirror. The sequences, automatic from so much visualization, flew from my body without thought. I felt prepared, but thinking about Dale's skill and age, along with the huge crowd, made my stomach roll. Alen caught me peeking out at the crowd, and gave his head a stern shake. I went back to my mirror.

Dale and I were fighting for the Canadian Champion Belt that night, so we fought last—the stars of the show. I could hear the familiar rowdy shouts and whistles from the crowd, and felt the energy start to fill my body. We danced into the ring as they announced us, both undefeated. The ref called us together to tap gloves.

"Let's have a clean fight, ladies." I stared up into Dale's eyes. She was slightly taller than me. Confidence oozed out of her. I could hardly stand still while the ref finished his little speech.

"They came to see a show, so let's give them one."

I slapped down on her gloves, just hard enough to make her glare at me. The extra-hard tap wasn't necessary, but I wanted her to know I was there. I was ready. The bell rang, and we went straight at each other, Dale with her long reach and powerful kicks, and me with my speed.

Chang and I knew that she could out power me, especially because I came in underweight, so our plan was outmaneuvering her. I had to attack quickly on the inside and get out, never staying in her sweet spot.

The first two rounds, I took my time, feeling out her style and patterns. She definitely had skill, by far the most talented fighter I'd faced so far. But she was slow. After one lumbering right hook, I dove in and landed five swift blows to her face. Her eyes flew open and she stumbled backward. The ref jumped between us and pushed me toward my corner. He held his hands up and started the eight-count.

"Are you okay? Can you see me?" Referees, to assess the coherence of a fighter, frequently use the standing eight-count. They have the power to call the fight right then, if they decide someone cannot continue. If they do—the other fighter is declared the winner by TKO.

Could this be over in the third round?

"Put your gloves up," he said at about the 6-second mark. "Can you continue?"

Sweat dripped off my nose while I stood and watched her regain her composure.

Oh, just go down already. Quit!

"Yeah. Yeah, I'm good," she managed, and the ref dropped his hands.

Crap.

She didn't quit, but she gave up some power in that moment. I knew I could at least stun her. Maybe a TKO was possible. The ref waved us back into the center, and I reignited my rapid combinations, calling it out in my head like an announcer.

Strong kick to the thigh, jab chest, uppercut chin. Good combo. Stay loose. Wait. Now! Right, left, kick to the stomach. Duck! Block! Jab, jab.

Round after round I attacked her. I landed so many kicks to her thighs, she couldn't even lift her leg to block. She was wounded, but she just would not fall. She was like a brick, and I was a twig swatting at her. By the last round,

I knew I had beaten her. But my mind started thinking ahead. *I have to get stronger.*

The ref grabbed our wrists and waited for the decision, but the crowd, on their feet and cheering, already knew the verdict. I looked at my father, who had finally stopped asking me to quit, grinning at my mother. I saw a group of teenagers from my school, many of whom I hardly knew, waving their arms at me. I glanced to my corner, and there was Alen, packing our things into a bag, just going about business as usual. For a moment, I wondered if he was disappointed that I didn't knock her out.

"And the winner, by unanimous decision, your new Canadian Kickboxing Champion—Leah Goldstein !"

February 3, 1985. Dale, age twenty-five, and I, age fifteen, fight for the Canadian Belt.

He pulled my arm up, and spun us in a circle, and I allowed myself a moment to smile, making sure to remove it before I turned back to Alen.

I knew I couldn't let up. Team Dale, as the newly unseated champion, was allowed to demand a rematch. And within minutes of my victory, that's exactly what they did. After the announcer had handed me the National Belt, and I had given my opponent the obligatory half hug, I looked over to her corner.

Her trainer and coach nodded at me—a quick acknowledgment of a good fight. Her husband, the other Dale, did not. His thin, red face puffed out from his white cotton team shirt. I suddenly remembered who he reminded me of—the devil in that freakishly scary church movie. He looked beyond angry, his pointy chin quivering, and suddenly he couldn't contain himself.

"This is not over! You can bet your ass there's going to be a rematch, and this time with some real judges!" He turned and glared and the announcers table. "You dumb fuckers have been doing this for twenty years, and you come up with that decision! Dammit, we just got FUCKED!"

The crowd, used to this kind of crude behavior, merely watched and laughed. But me, who had never uttered a single swear word in my life, was appalled that someone could be so low-class. Alen could sense my unease, and turned me out of the auditorium and back through the lobby of the hotel. Dale came behind, still slinging insults and profanity. In the hallway, Alen couldn't take it anymore.

He spun to face him. "You want rematch? Okay!" he

blurted. "We fight you. Anytime!" I'd never seen Alen even remotely upset, and here he was, a tiny Chinese pacifist yelling back and forth with an ill-tempered buffoon. I think Dale was just in shock. He had predicted an easy victory, and the fight hadn't gone how he'd planned. The only way he knew how to deal with it was rant. Alen absorbed several more minutes of insults, always yelling back "Okay! Anytime!" Maybe that's all he felt he needed to say, or maybe his poor English prohibited him from creating better comebacks. Either way, he quickly grew weary of the yelling match. He spun my shoulder around and we walked back toward our hotel rooms.

"I think we just made enemy," he whispered.

We glanced at each other, a slightly amused look on his face. I raised my eyebrows, "I think you're right." *Bring it on.*

My parents, Alen, and a few friends went out to eat to celebrate. I was starving. I had hardly eaten all day, partly from nerves, and partly in an effort to stay light. *Stay fast.* My stomach growled, as I looked at the plate of fries in the middle of the table.

"Eat some," my mother urged. "Your fight is over."

I had to give her credit, she'd put up with my food craziness for years. She'd watched me weigh, measure, and count everything that went in my mouth. I thought about what I had written down yesterday.

½ Apple

1 Banana

10 Crackers

7 oz. Salmon

2 cups Steamed Broccoli

1 Boiled Egg

1 Pear

And today, I've eaten less than half that. I deserve some fries ...

Everyone talked over each other, laughing and eating. I tried to enjoy the moment, but I couldn't turn off my internal calculator.

One fry is probably 20 calories, so I can only eat five, if I'm going to eat the fish I ordered. One bite of that—25 calories. Only eat half of that. Unless you're going to run tomorrow. Yeah, I should run.

In the end, I ate about five fries, but ended up vomiting an hour later at home. It could've been that my body was so unaccustomed to fried food that it just rejected it, or it could've been my subconscious deliberately punishing me for breaking my food rules. Either way, I didn't eat another French fry until I was forty-three.

The next morning, my sixteenth birthday, I strolled into Service Canada to take my driving test. My cheek was puffy, and I had the beginnings of a black eye, but really, I'd looked much worse from tough training matches. Still, the overweight, oily-haired employee grimaced when he saw my face. He ushered me to a tiny hatchback and I went through my checklist while he wedged himself into the passenger's seat.

Hands at 10 and 2, always shoulder check, use your blinker, do NOT mess this up!

My license would mean freedom. My mother didn't

drive, so most of my car rides were on my father's Saturday hunts for potential property. I wasn't interested in real estate at all; I just liked to ride. I wanted my license so much, my heart was racing and my palms were sweaty. *Was I this nervous last night?* I couldn't remember.

I ended up completing the entire route just fine, except for the part where I almost hit a pedestrian. I had to hit the brakes quite hard and my greasy instructor had to brace himself against the dashboard. I chastised myself all the way back, sure that I'd failed. He didn't say a word to me as we walked back inside.

"Wait here." He pointed at a group of black chairs. Minutes later, he came back with my Learner's Permit. I couldn't believe it.

"I saw you fight last night—you were amazing."

My mouth dropped. "Oh yeah? Thanks. It was pretty good, I guess."

We chatted for a few more minutes, me assuring him that I would fight even better next time, and that I'd watch out for pedestrians.

Two days after swearing off French fries and driving my father's car way more than necessary, I went right back to my routine. However, my enthusiasm for driving frightened me. I was terrified of getting lazy, and I knew whatever I had done so far was working—I hadn't lost a fight. So I added yet another rule to my growing list of training conditions: I must run at least six miles or workout for an hour, before getting into a car.

I also added strength training to my three-a-day workout

regime, lifting weights at our local YMCA. I had only been going to school part time for over a year, completing courses through correspondence. The additional training made me more obsessive about time, not wanting to waste a second. I spent the last half hour before bedtime preparing for my next day. My three sets of training clothes all laid out with the corresponding shoes; runners next to my shorts, handwraps lying on my sweats, and a third set of gear for my night training with Alen.

I'd prep most of my food, plan all of my school time, and even put toothpaste on my toothbrush—all to save precious seconds the next morning. Whenever I felt like slacking off, I thought about Dale, and his arrogant, goateed face. The next time I met his wife, who didn't seem nearly as enthusiastic as her husband, I wouldn't leave it in the judges' hands.

Within a few months, I could feel the power of my punches move to another level. We always wore headgear in training, but a few guys started to shake their heads after sparring with me. I grinned, knowing I was finally making their heads roll too.

"Good job, Leah," said Gavin, as he peeled off his gloves at the end of evening training. "I think I saw stars on that last one." I nodded, smiling only on the inside. "Are you coming to watch us on Saturday?"

The boxing card that weekend included three guys from our gym. "Of course. Good luck," I managed. The guys respected me, and several tried to get closer, as friends or more. But I always kept my distance. While other teenagers went on dates and went through their first breakups, I trained. I lifted weights, I ran until I puked, I slammed my fists into heavy bags, but I had no desire to date. At all.

I considered a few people from school as friends, along with the boxing guys, but I could not even imagine one of them as a boyfriend. The thought of someone even holding my hand made my skin crawl, and watching girls sob about some boy who just broke up with her baffled me. *How could anyone matter that much?*

I thought teenagers in general, were ridiculous—smoking and drinking and trying to talk over each other in the hallway. I rolled my eyes listening to them brag about their drunken weekend and who they "hooked up" with. If someone even hinted that they were interested in me, I had plenty of excuses on hand. "I'm way too busy training to think about that right now," "Oh, my parents are really strict; I wouldn't be allowed," or my favorite, while pointing to my latest fat lip, "Who'd want to date me?"

I decided to support my boxing buddies though, and headed to a crappy community center in Richmond to watch the Saturday night fights. I had dragged my friend, Sharon, along with me, although I feared the rough crowd would scare the crap out of her. I decided that she was too sheltered, and talked her into coming with me.

Sharon sat behind me in algebra, one of the only required courses I still went to school for. Her frumpy clothes, Chinese accent, and thick glasses made her an easy target for the popular kids. She kept her eyes down in class and rarely said a word. My contempt for the normal teenage diet of drinking, parties, and soap-opera relationships was at an all-time high, and although many of those popular kids wanted to be friends with me, I shunned them. I thought they were immature and mean, and one day, as Sharon looked more withdrawn than ever, I spun around and asked her if she wanted to walk to McDonald's with me after school.

Her eyes shot open, and stared at me over her glasses that had slid down her nose. "Umm, okay," was all she could manage. And then, walking over the Burrard Bridge after school, we ran into some rough Grade Twelves from another high school. The three girls and one guy walked shoulder-to-shoulder right at us. The narrow sidewalk ran directly adjacent to the busy four-lane street; it was impossible to pass them. We were trapped.

"Hey, where ya going?" the obvious leader asked.

Her three friends laughed and stepped closer, making it clear that they wouldn't hesitate to pound us. I heard a small whimper from Sharon. I stepped in front of her, lifting my hands slightly, and widening my stance.

"What are you going to do?" I challenged. "I have a black belt and I'm a professional kickboxer. Want me to prove it?" The energy shifted as the leader took a half step back. She considered it. I'd never used my training to fight anyone outside a ring, except once. An oversized grade-school bully used to pick on kids during recess. He picked on me one day, and I paid him back with a turning kick to the head. The principal saw me through the window and motioned with his finger to come to his office. It was totally worth the stern lecture.

The group didn't move, so I took another step forward.

Suddenly, Sharon, surging with newfound power, yelled, "Kick her ass, Leah! I got your back!" I turned to see her shuffling her feet with her hands up by her face. I had to stifle my smile as I turned back to the "gangsters." They had already turned to walk away. We laughed all the way to McDonald's, where Sharon celebrated with a Big Mac and fries, and I had my usual Diet Coke.

Sharon turned out to be the daughter of the Chinese consul, and a black belt, with extremely protective, over-achieving parents. She couldn't go anywhere without a bodyguard except school, so she had to sneak out to come with me to the boxing match. Her shy demeanor seemed to melt away as we walked along the busy streets.

"Thanks for inviting me, Leah." She pulled some snacks out of her purse, and handed me a pepperoni stick. "They're made with ostrich, try it," she said, knowing I didn't eat pork or beef.

I was still taking little nibbles of it as we walked into the Richmond Community Center. It was too salty, but I thought throwing it away would be rude, so I continued to carry it. I spotted Gavin across the gym and started toward him, when I heard a man's voice behind me.

"Maybe you shouldn't eat all of that, Leah. Looking a little hefty there."

It was Dale. Again. *The boxing world is way too small.* Sharon looked desperately at the ground. My face went flush, knowing his comments might be hurting my shy, overweight friend more than me. I didn't respond.

"Maybe you should be fighting welterweight."

His put-downs were completely unnecessary. My weight obsession, like all boxers to some degree, was always front-of-mind. I didn't need his assistance.

I grabbed Sharon's arm, "Let's go." We turned and continued to the bleachers. As we sat, Sharon turned to me.

"You know you're not fat, Leah."

"Yeah, I know," I said, shaking my head and rolling my eyes.

I did. I knew. And my desire to stay thin had nothing to do with vanity. I never looked at myself in the mirror nor did I care what people thought about my body. Staying thin was all about performance. *Thin is fast.* Dale's comment, just like all of his ridiculous yelling at our match, merely gave me fuel. For months, I kept his voice in my head as I battered the heavy bag. *Just wait until the rematch. I'll show you how fat I am.*

I waltzed into the Royal Towers Hotel with my head higher and my body stronger than eight months ago, and this time, confidence oozed out of me. The billboards along the highway and around the hotel were plastered with Dale's face, her taped hands held close to her cheeks. I couldn't help but smile. *Wow—somebody's manager really wants some publicity.* The peeling wallpaper around the conference room curled out from behind huge posters and banners. They all carried some form of the same message. *Go, Dale. Kick Leah's ass.* Not one poster for me, and I was glad. They seemed desperate and phony. *I don't need a stupid poster to knock her out.*

I warmed up, listening to five hundred people calling our

names. Other fights led up to ours, but no one seemed to care. They wanted to see the grudge match. I skipped rope and stretched, turning my thoughts inward. I put my heel up on the wall and pressed into the splits, my hips loose and strong. Alen slowly wrapped my hands, calm and methodical. I could hear his coaching voice in my head. *Keep your energy to yourself. Every ounce of strength you have should be used only to fight. Nothing else.*

I shadow boxed in the mirror and pictured Dale falling to the mat.

Alen pointed at my bag. It was time. I went into the locker room and changed into my fighting clothes, new black kung fu-style shirt with a Canadian and Israeli flag, and my "Praying Mantis" t-shirt that still hid half my thin arms. I leaned on the sink and stared into the mirror. *This is your sport. You've been saving it all up for today. Time to let it go.*

I could hear Dale's music blaring as she skipped through the crowd to the ring. I was the champion, so I would be announced second. Alen rubbed Vaseline across both my cheeks and slid on my gloves. He put in my mouth guard, held my hands together, and locked me in a stare. I realized that we were exactly the same height. He nodded and I nodded back. Words were unnecessary; we both knew what was coming.

I put my hands on his shoulders, looked at the ground, and followed him out into the noise. I never looked up, and the whistles and yelling became more muffled as we neared our corner. I stepped into the ring and addressed the crowd—a quick spin and thank you wave to each corner. And then I turned to the Dales. The crowd noise lowered further, as though water was filling my ears and muffling everything. I could only see and hear the target. Even Alen slid into the background.

The ref called us together, and I waited for a feeling of déjà vu. The scene was exactly the same. Same fighters. Same peeling wallpaper. Same yelling crowd, ref's speech, coaches in the corners, and judges' table. It all appeared identical. Except it wasn't. She knew it and I knew it. The ref rambled on about etiquette and clean fighting, while I glared at her.

This is my sport, and you will not make it through this bout.

She blinked, too many times. I knew she was scared, and I had to wonder if she even wanted to be a fighter. Her husband was the pompous idiot, trying to make "them" famous in the kickboxing world, not her. In the moment, ready to fight, however, I could not afford to separate them. Dale was Dale. And I hated them both.

By the time the bell rang, I could only hear my breath. I felt my gloves brush against each other as I stepped out to meet her, my lungs slowly filling with air. I didn't hesitate, and lunged forward. I landed six solid punches to the ribs and face, the last one with a satisfying crunch on her nose and I knew that it was broken. I gave her no time to recover and hammered into her ribs. I threw my weight into an uppercut to her belly, and she dropped to one knee.

I wasn't happy or relieved. I didn't hope she'd stay down. I was possessed. *Get up. Get up so we can continue this.* She slowly got back on her feet, the ref holding her hands up for a moment. I saw her nod weakly as the ref stepped out of the way. I launched myself into a turning kick, spun, and landed my right foot squarely into her left thigh. By far, the hardest kick I'd ever delivered, and tears sprang to her eyes. I waited about 10 seconds, and then hammered her right thigh. She threw a few punches, but her stance had changed, and I knew her legs were finished.

If you've never been kicked in the outer thigh, it's nearly impossible to explain the pain. It's excruciating, and worse, you lose muscle control. I knew she was hurting in several places, and she couldn't kick. I saw her left arm drop slightly. I swung a right hook to her temple and watched her head spin, pulling her body along for the ride. She slid down the ropes and onto the floor. Ding. *Saved by the bell.*

Alen spoke while he wiped my forehead with a towel, but I couldn't hear him. I didn't need to hear him. I watched Dale's corner scurrying around, trying to motivate her by demonstrating blocks and countermoves. But her eyes were flat. I knew she was done. The bell rang leading us into the second round, and I repeated the opening of the fight. I went straight at her with strong punches to the face and ribs, as she stumbled backwards and fell to the mat. I glanced to her corner, and saw the white towel skidding into the ring. *Knockout.*

Husband Dale and a few others helped her out of the ring and straight out of the hotel. I knew she would never fight again. I stood alone in the ring, as they announced me as the defending National Champion. The cheering and clapping from the standing crowd gradually made its way into my blocked ears. I could finally hear them, and it was deafening. The ref handed me the title belt, and I held it over my head for a final spin. I exhaled slowly, grateful for the moment. I ducked under the ropes and followed Alen right back out, already thinking about the next step: the World Championship.

Defending Canadian Champion

I walked into the gym the next day; Alen was just finishing sweeping the floor.

"What are you doing here?" he asked, wide-eyed and slightly amused.

"I'm here to train," I stated simply. Several of us had fought the night before, and it was understood that we would all take a day or two off. But I couldn't. Alen knew it was pointless to try to change my mind.

"Okay. Do some skipping and hit the light bag for about twenty minutes. Then go home. I'm going to eat."

He went through the back door, leading into his family's apartment over the gym. I turned back to the mirror and grabbed my jump rope. I swung it around slowly at first, shifting my weight front to back and side to side. I crossed and uncrossed my arms as I floated through the beaded rope, every movement second nature.

The smell of the spicy Chinese food started creeping through the vent and my stomach growled. I faced the mirror and swung the rope faster, running in place, my toes hardly brushing the floor. I switched to double jumps, the beads ticking the floor twice every time I jumped. I skipped faster and harder, pounding my feet into the floor, feeling sweat build on my forehead.

I switched to the speed bag. The movement seemed to wave the appetizing aromas right into my face. My stomach protested again. I hit the bag faster and harder. I switched to the heavy bag, working around it like an opponent, darting in for an attack, and ducking imaginary counterpunches. I worked and worked until the smells had subsided and my stomach was silent. I looked at the clock. I'd been there two and a half hours.

That's why I'm the best. I out-trained everyone, even the other guys at my gym. I would fight for the World Kickboxing Association title within a year, and I wanted to be able to give myself the same pep talk I had for all my previous fights. *Nobody works harder than me. I deserve to win.* It was that simple. I believed my extreme training allowed me to dominate the sport; I couldn't let up. There was always more training I could do.

I dry-heaved. The combination of the heat and the steep inclines made my stomach burn. The road seemed to bulge and constrict under my bike, like I was riding over waves of pavement that just wouldn't settle. I couldn't believe the heat was affecting me so much. *I lived in Israel for ten years!* I wobbled into a barely-lit dirt parking lot. Sean caught my bike, and Lori and Connie slid their arms under mine.

"What time is it?" I mumbled.

"One in the morning," Lori answered. The three of us stumbled into a motel room, arm in arm in arm. Two cowboy statues stood on the bedside table, surrounded by Gatorade, ice tea, Diet Pepsi, Snapple—practically every drink I could think of. Apparently, Janessa and Ed had radioed ahead, warning them.

"Leah, you have to drink more," Connie offered. "If you get more dehydrated, you're risking the race."

"I know." *I know!* I just didn't feel like it. Perhaps I was beyond thirsty. I sipped orange Gatorade while they peeled off my gloves and shoes.

I took a quick shower, rubbing my fingers over my swollen, chapped lips. *Gotta keep on the sunscreen.* I came back into the empty room and lay down. After a quick rap on the door, Rob came in with his medical kit.

"Oh shit, am I dying?" I joked.

He calmly smiled. "Not yet." He pulled out an IV line and a bag of saline. "I think you need one of these, though." I turned my head away as he skillfully slid the needle into my shriveled vein. "You'll feel better after all that goes in."

"Promise? Because I could sue you if this doesn't work."

"Ah, still have your sense of humor. That's a good sign. Go to sleep." He gently closed the door.

Thank God, we brought a medic.

Alen and I planned out my final year of competition. The World Championship fight was eleven months away. I need-ed another fight to stay sharp. Alen put the word out that I was looking for a match. And wouldn't you know it, Dale the promoter found a U.S. fighter to face me. Female kickboxers were scarce, and skilled ones even more so. Neither Alen nor I trusted Dale, but really had no choice but to agree. We asked Dale for some video of her, not an unusual request at the time. But of course, no video was available.

Alen asked other coaches and managers if they'd seen this girl fight. No one had ever heard of her. My suspicions grew, as I continued to train for my ghost opponent. Then, one week before the match, Dale called and informed us that the girl was injured and couldn't fight, but we shouldn't worry, because he'd already found a replacement.

I knew it. What a snake. He didn't want me to have time to prepare, so he planned this from the beginning. The boxing card next Saturday was full. I was the main event, fighting at the biggest venue of my career. Newspapers and magazines had promoted the fights all month. Dale knew I wouldn't withdraw.

I could have. It was at my discretion, but I still needed the practice fight, and so Alen and I showed up for the morning weigh-in. I walked into the PNE (Pacific National Exhibition) Gardens unsure and nervous; I felt feverish and had a sore throat, just the beginnings of a big cold. I had a chill, so I wore my sweatshirt and running shoes up onto the scale, knowing I was underweight anyway. Just as I stepped off, a six-foot woman strolled into the locker room wearing nothing but a sports bra and underwear. Dale came in right behind her.

"I didn't know there was another female fight tomorrow. Who is she fighting?" I asked the weigh-in judge.

"You," he replied, raising one eyebrow. Boxing is known for dirty promoters, setting up mismatches, and not paying fighters. He was merely conveying that this was one of those times. I had always demanded payment up front for my fights—I'd already been paid for this one. So Dale had gotten me back another way. A giant.

I watched her step on the scale: 170 pounds. I spun around to Alen, eyes wide. He said nothing.

"Don't worry, she'll cut more weight. We'll put her in the sauna for a while," offered her coach.

"Yeah, don't worry," grinned Dale.

How stupid do you think I am?

"So, she's going to sit in the sauna for three hours—and lose fifty pounds!" I yelled. I'd never raised my voice around officials. It took Dale by surprise. "What is she going to do, amputate a leg?"

Alen stepped between us and pushed me across the room.

"You don't have to fight her. It still up to you," he whispered.

I breathed once, slowly. "What do you think, Alen? Could I still beat her?"

"Yes, I think so. But it still up to you."

As we walked out, I told Dale the fight was still on.

"Don't worry, we'll stay here and weigh her again," he said.

"Yeah, you do that."

The PNE Gardens sits just east of downtown Vancouver; so needless to say, most of the crowd was on my side. In fact, when they announced my opponent, I heard a wave of boos and jeers. I'd like to think that the savvy crowd could see a mismatch when they saw one, but it could be that half my high school was there and they were louder than anyone else. My throat and joints throbbed as I made my way to the ring. But still, I tuned out the crowd and focused on the giant, staring at her collarbones as we stood across from each other. Her muscles bulged in her arms and legs.

Gotta be quick tonight.

Stay on the inside. Don't let her get a full swing in. Take out her legs. That's all I had. I knew nothing about her.

From the start, I peppered her with shots to the chin, gut, and ribs; all of them felt like I was punching a tree. I worked her legs, kicked her stomach, and landed good shots to her temples, all the while avoiding her huge, heavy swings. Through the first five rounds, she had fallen four times. But each time, clambered back onto her feet. *Crap.* I sat in my corner, my father next to me for first time. He and Alen seemed relaxed; after all, I would definitely win by decision as long as I didn't get knocked out. But I didn't want another decision.

I came out faster in the sixth and last round. I threw my weight into her face and ribs, willing her to go down. She dropped her hands slightly, and I landed three solid shots to her nose. She slid down to a knee. The ref started the standing eight-count while I prayed for a finish. The ref finally waved his hands.

Thank God. I waved in a quick turn to the crowd and ducked out of the arena. I couldn't wait to get home and go to bed. I was sure I'd be sicker the next day.

I never did really get sick after that fight, and went right back to training. I felt a bit run down, but not even a snowstorm the next day kept me from the gym. I had six months until the World Title fight. I couldn't waste a day. Only Homeless Todd and I showed up. Todd, at least 40 pounds heavier than me, had joined the gym a few months prior. Alen never charged any of us for coaching, and although I'm sure my parents gave him something, many of the guys trained for free. I'm not sure how Todd came to be on the streets at eighteen years old, but he never complained about anything. He was a good street fighter, and Alen was slowly turning him into a kickboxer. But he was still very inexperienced and not someone I would normally spar with.

"Well, this is it," announced Alen. "You two spar."

I felt apprehensive at first, but Todd seemed cautious and controlled. Rookie fighters make mistakes, they punch too hard or move in unpredictable patterns, and injuries are more common. As we eased into the first few minutes, though, I relaxed. Todd was good. I backed him into the corner, popping his headgear with jabs. Suddenly, he wrapped his arms around my shoulders. It's a common move in boxing, just to catch your breath; you lean on your opponent where they can't punch you. Normally, I would have pushed him back and continued. But in that moment, I heard a loud snap in my back and I fell to the mat.

An electrical current surged down into my legs as I rolled onto my side.

Am I paralyzed? Oh God, I can't move my legs!

Todd started to panic.

"Are you okay, Leah? Get up! C'mon, you're okay," as if saying it would somehow make it true.

I tried to stay calm, as Alen rubbed Chinese oils on my back, trying to ease the incredible pain. *Six months. I only have six months.* I stayed there for over half an hour, the side of my face lying on the dirty mat. The pain didn't let up, and I finally decided I might as well lie in pain at home. The guys helped me to my feet, Todd apologizing and asking if he could help me. I assured him I'd be fine. I shuffled to my car, wincing every step, and wedged myself into the driver's seat. My hips wouldn't bend, so I had to recline my seat into a Lazy-Boy position and reach out for the steering wheel like a wannabe-gangster. My mother took me, after a sleepless night (by bus, of course, since she still didn't drive) to the hospital. X-rays showed a herniated disc.

At first, the doctor implied surgery was our only option. My mother refused. She never did believe in the traditional medical system. I panicked, asking what I could do. He suggested a few months of total rest, and then another X-ray. I couldn't stand the thought of missing my fight or lying around for eight weeks. I begged him for a physiotherapy referral, and he reluctantly agreed. I drove straight to her office, and an athletic-looking lady with red hair and an Irish accent came out to meet me. She was skeptical after looking at my X-ray and discussing my situation.

"This is a very serious injury, Leah. I know this upcoming fight is important, but so is your long-term health."

I spoke fast. "I heal really fast. I'll do whatever you tell me to do. I know I can come back from this."

"Okay, let's see what we can do," she smiled.

I relished the traction and exercises, because even though they were painful, I knew every appointment would get me closer to the World Championship fight. After a week, though, nothing seemed to be happening. I still shuffled when I walked, the pain kept me up all night, and my fitness plan still said, "Rest." My doctor and physio still thought I should take it easy, but I just didn't believe them. I thought movement would heal my back faster, plus I knew I was losing precious cardiovascular training, so I headed out to the seawall, a seemingly endless path splitting the city of Vancouver from the Pacific Ocean.

In the beginning, my pace was pathetic. Old men with

canes would pass me and nod sympathetically, as I winced and slid my feet forward. My shuffle gradually became an upright walk, and exactly two weeks after my injury, my walk turned into a jog. I could feel my back and legs getting stronger every day, so it took me by surprise when my physio sat me down and told me what she really thought.

"Leah, I know in the beginning you believed that you'd be able to fight in a few months, but that's just not going to happen. You probably won't ever even kickbox again. But you're athletic, I'm sure there are other sports you'll be able to do. Have you ever tried swimming?"

She was serious. I stared at her, stunned; my mouth gaped open. I thought she believed in me, but really she'd just been placating me like a child.

I stood up. "I guess there's no reason for me to come here then."

She called after me, but I kept walking. She didn't believe in me and just like my doctor, had to be abandoned.

I rehabbed myself, running the seawall, and slowly adding strength training and shadowboxing. The pain, terrible in the first few months, slowly improved enough for a return to the gym. I sparred with Alen while he perfectly mimicked my upcoming opponent, the current World Champion from New Mexico, Arlene Weber. The blocks and countermoves became automatic. I smashed my fists into Gavin's head and ribs, picturing the ref grabbing my right hand and pulling it into the air. I trained harder than ever, knowing only two things to be true; in four months, I would face my toughest opponent ever, and this would be my very last fight.

Over the past six months, my headaches had gradually got worse, especially after a tough sparring match. I also had trouble speaking sometimes, as if the word I wanted to say was stuck in my throat, and just wouldn't come out. We wore protective headgear when sparring, but I knew the blows were taking a toll. I knew my symptoms were caused by the training, and I knew it was time to stop—after one final fight.

I obsessed about retiring with a perfect record, while Alen started thinking about my next career: movies. Hong Kong producers sent me for photo shoots and screen tests, sure I could be a big star in Asian kung fu movies. Alen pushed me.

"Little blonde-haired girl with your moves? You be big hit! Make lot of money."

I nodded and followed along, and although the producers and Alen were very serious about my potential movie career, I never was. I had known my life path since I was four years old: military, Mossad, flying car with guns on the sides. Nowhere in my life fantasies had I pictured myself in a kung fu movie, beating up pretend bad guys with right hooks and flying kicks, and then heading home to cook dinner for my boyfriend wearing nothing but my bra and underwear.

Who writes this crap? I tossed the script to my bedroom floor. I had promised Alen I would read it, and I did. *And now I have to tell him that there's no way I'd agree to any of these. Partial nudity? I can't even expose my stomach without feeling embarrassed.*

I laced up my running shoes. I wanted to get some sprints done before it rained. My feet slapped the cement as I wondered why the nudity bothered me so much.

I had finally gotten over my Jesus-phase. Although after the scary church movie and my belief that he had healed my stray dog, Schultzy, it took years before I even questioned him. My family didn't go to synagogue, and I only had a few Sundays of over-the-top Christian education to go on, so my religious knowledge was limited. I still believed in God though, and I was sure that nudity, even for a film, would be considered a sin. But even beyond that, I simply hated the idea of being that exposed to anyone, and I began to wonder if something was wrong with me.

I jogged into our neighborhood park, and with the warm-up over, sprinted down the tree-lined path at top speed. I leaned forward and let my heels kick back, taking long, fast strides. I turned at the corner and picked up speed, charging along the path, trying to turn off my thoughts and just focus on my legs. I felt like I was flying. *I will be known as a great athlete and not a poor student. I will be remembered as a World Champion kickboxer, and not the shy girl who was a total loner. I will be perfect.* After all, that's what the Mossad would be looking for. Perfection. I couldn't allow any flaws.

I swung my arms into the last 100 meters, my heart pounding in my ears. A woman and a dog stood at the end of the path, and as I approached I could tell that she was staring at me. I slowed as I recognized her. It was my redheaded physiotherapist, marveling no doubt that I could sprint like that. I walked toward her as she stuttered.

"Wow, Leah. I've been following you in the papers. I guess you're going to fight?"

"Yeah. I told you I would. You know, you should be careful what you say to people—deciding what's possible for them. Just imagine if I had believed you."

She nodded, and I broke back into a sprint.

Connie sprinted alongside me, spraying me with cold water. "Is that as fast as you can go, Leah?" she egged me on.

Apparently we've resorted to insults to push me up hills. Lori picked up where she left off and jogged beside me. "Ya look good," she lied.

"I feel good," I lied back.

"I'll race you to the top!" she yelled and broke into a sprint. The crest of the hill was only about fifty yards away and she had a head start, but I couldn't let that go. I dropped a couple gears and stood up, pushing my legs to go faster. I quickly closed the distance and passed her just before the top.

"Lucky!" she breathed.

"Not in a million years would I lose that race!" I yelled back. I can't help but compete. It's what I do.

My father drove me to the PNE on fight night and I couldn't think of any small talk, so I sat in silence as we weaved through the Saturday traffic. I concentrated on slow breaths but surprisingly, I didn't feel nervous. I felt like a seasoned musician who still gets excited to perform, but doesn't have to think about forgetting the words to a song. I was a professional, and this was just another fight. A few blocks from the arena, my father slowed for pedestrians jaywalking in the street. The crowd got thicker and thicker as we neared the arena and only after we'd eased our way through the throngs to the side door did it dawn on me that all these people were here to see me.

This is the World Championships, Leah. My stomach did a small flip. It was exhilarating to see so many people pouring through the door, but I didn't have one bit of nervous energy. I knew I would win, and move on to my next goal. I didn't think the fight would be easy—Alen and I had studied a few videos of the current titleholder's previous bouts.

"Arlene Weber fight clean and tough. Just like man. Just like you," Alen had said, pointing at the screen. He was right. I watched, and took mental notes on her attack tendencies, and how her hands lagged when she fatigued. She was very good. But I knew I was better. By the time Alen shoved in my mouth guard and I put my hands on his shoulders to walk to the ring, there wasn't a doubt in my mind that I owned this sport.

I don't even remember much about the actual fight, except that punching her head felt like hitting a bowling ball. I hit her hard—as hard as I could—but she shook off every blow. The fight went a full seven rounds, and was the best fight I'd ever had—clean and fast. The huge crowd stood on their feet the whole time, screaming and clapping, and as the last bell rang, started chanting my name. Arlene gave me a hug.

"Congratulations. You deserve it."

That night, I lay on my bed and stared at the ceiling. *I'm the World Champion. Me. The World Champion. I did it.* My body, strangely relaxed and heavy, didn't feel like my own. I'd spent years tense—prepping and planning and training. The stillness unnerved me. I breathed slowly, my hands tucked under my head. *So, you're the World Champion.* I grinned. *Wrinkles be damned.*

"What are you smiling at, Leah?" Sean shouted at me.

The van pulled up right beside me. I glanced over and shook my head.

"You have to eat something! It's been hours!"

He was right. But the heat was making me nauseous and I could hardly think about a piece of Power Bar or a Hammer Gel without dry heaving. *How many more days of this?*

"I'll just have some apples."

Sean reluctantly handed me a ziplock full of cut-up apples.

"You have to eat some protein too, ya know!"

I waved him off with my hand, and they fell back behind me. I propped my left elbow on the handlebars and held the bag, and ate with my right. I forced a few pieces down, making sure they saw me swallow. Finally, the van sped around me and resumed leapfrogging. With no eyes babysitting me anymore, I shoved the apples into my back jersey pocket. *I'll eat more later. Maybe.*

Colorado

"Everything you've ever wanted is on the other side of fear."
George Addair

The glorious Rocky Mountains loomed ahead of me, and while most riders may dread this part of the race, I looked forward to it. I love to climb. I threw my weight forward and stood on the pedals, a welcome break for my bum.

"Hey, Leah, we just heard Caroline has pulled out. She lasted less than forty-eight hours," Ed came through my earpiece.

Wow. I guess it doesn't matter how prepared a rider is—ya just never know what will happen.

"I guess she didn't like the heat, eh, Leah?" Ed laughed. He knows I love riding in hot weather. *But Death Valley was even a bit beyond my limit.* "You are on record-breaking pace. Keep it up!"

I nodded, and felt a small surge of pain in my neck. *This helmet is actually starting to feel kind of heavy. Probably should've done those neck exercises my physiotherapist told me to do.*

I laughed to myself. *It'll be fine.*

I finished high school mostly by correspondence, and worked at Spa Lady, a women's only fitness center in Richmond. I lied about my age to get the job, and quickly became a manager. Spa Lady upper management required a quota of new memberships to be filled each month, and no one was better at it than me. Almost anyone who walked in off the street walked out with a lifetime membership. I made a commission off each sale, so I simply didn't take "no" for an answer. It kept me busy while I bided my time—as soon as I graduated, I could move to Israel.

I practiced rope climbs and ran sprints at the track preparing for the military, physically and mentally. *I have to be more than perfect.* I didn't really have any close friends, and although people from school often invited me to join them at a movie or a party, I rarely deviated from my work, school, and workout schedule. Finally, my diploma arrived, and I moved to Israel, gratefully flying toward the first step of my life's dream.

The first few months flew by, setting up a bedroom in my aunt's house and going to interviews. Most recruits spend at least some time being questioned by the military. They want to know your history, your strengths, your weaknesses, and have an idea of which specialty you're suited for. With my athletic background, I thought it was likely that I'd be slated into something physically demanding—but all I hoped for was the quickest path to the secret service.

The morning of my recruitment day, my father drove me down to the bus terminal near Tel Aviv. He had flown over to Israel with me, not because I needed help (I'd been flying solo to Israel since I was twelve), but to visit his family and make sure I had everything I needed for boot camp. I could feel my father's energy. He was fearful of how the military would exploit me, and couldn't for the life of him understand why I would volunteer for this. My excitement, not hindered in the least, made me squirm and strain my neck to see more of the milling crowd.

The military buses were new and clean, and it almost felt like we were headed to summer camp. The families of the other girls stood alongside my dad and watched us all find our seats. The tears were still flowing from many faces as the bus started up. The drama seemed almost comical to me. Mothers and daughters clutching each other and saying goodbye between sobs was just a little too much. This particular group had been selected to undergo an abbreviated basic training, indicating that they had something special about them. The military saw something in us that was superior to the average recruit—and I expected everyone to be made of rock (just as I thought I was). Besides, they all knew this day was coming—everyone in Israel is required to serve a minimum amount in the military. And it wasn't like we were going to war or anything—it was just basic training. How bad could it be?

Almost as soon as the bus pulled away from our waving families, we started to find out. The officers walked down the aisle belittling and insulting anyone they could. I was prepared for this. I knew the hard treatment from the "higher-ups" was all part of the programming to make us tough. I already felt tough, and didn't feel the least bit intimidated or afraid. I may have been the only one, as sobs and sniffling continued along our bus ride. An officer approached a crying girl at the front and said, "Since you are crying like that, I have to assume someone just died!

When, like fifteen minutes ago? Who was it, your brother or something? You had better save your tears—you'll need lots of them for what you're going to do." Crap like that. She made her way down the rows warning everyone of what torture lay ahead. "No more make-up. No more boyfriends. You're nobody! You're just a number now!"

She eventually made her way back to me. I was wearing my favorite black Ray Bans, and feeling pretty confident and calm. She yanked my sunglasses off and said, "What is this? Are you a goddamn tourist? You look a little too happy with yourself—what do you think this is? The bus to Disneyland!" I had been warned by older family members that this was going to happen. I'm sure most new recruits got some sort of pep talk from their older siblings or cousins on how to take abuse without reacting. You're expected to keep your eyes forward and listen, without frowning, crying, smiling, or—heaven forbid—laughing. She continued, "Nice hair. Are you visiting from Sweden or something?" I had to admit, she kinda got me. I did look like a tourist. I liked my dyed blonde hair, cargo pants, and sweet sunglasses—but I knew it was all about to be stripped away.

We arrived at the base like cattle—pouring off buses into the unknown. Before getting on the bus in Ramat Gan, we were warned to leave behind all personal items. Translation: Other than the clothes on your back, don't bring one freaking thing with you to basic training! And we didn't. We were thrown a huge duffel bag and started shuffling through an endless series of lines to collect our gear. We received six uniforms—four combat (working) and two dress (for ceremonies and leave), two pairs of boots, t-shirts, socks, and underwear.

Amid the shouts and torments from the officers, we shoved in toiletries, sunscreen, chamois cream to prevent chafing, and all of our bedding. The teardrop-shaped duffle gradually got heavier and heavier, and when full, was taller than some of the girls. Many of them had to drag their bags over to the barracks. The bus ride in had only been about thirty minutes, but to gather all that gear for seventy new recruits took over two hours.

I adjusted easily into military life. Running in the deep sand, getting yelled at, and surviving sleep deprivation while difficult, still didn't deter my enthusiasm for fitness. I often snuck into the showers in the middle of the night just to shadowbox and do push-ups. I wanted to be superior physically and, to me, that meant training harder than everyone else. I ran the obstacle course during my free time, just to ensure that at test time I would break the record. I did.

During boot camp (Base 12), commanders continued to create profiles of the incoming soldiers. My report probably said, "Great motivation, physically superior, doesn't work well with others." Our platoons would be given group "missions" and just the thought of relying on others for my success stressed me out. I never openly complained or bailed on an assignment, but I'm sure my superiors could tell I worked better alone. These factors, plus I'm sure my martial arts background, shot me straight to the fitness hub of the military, Base 8.

Bootcamp

Behind Wingate, a university near Netanya, this secure base is charged with training soldiers in fitness, shooting, and hand-to-hand combat. Krav Maga, perhaps the most well-known and revered aspect of the Israeli military, prepares soldiers to fight with their hands and bodies rather than relying on weapons. Most of the maneuvers involve a defensive movement, followed quickly by a potentially lethal attack. Subduing or injuring an opponent is never the goal.

I learned about weapons, gas, and combat maneuvers during the day, and still trained myself at night. One early morning, I slid under the base fence so I could run on the university track. As I stood, a young lieutenant was walking straight at me. *Oh, crap.* Leaving the base was absolutely forbidden—he could've arrested me—and visions of my father standing in knee-deep water flashed through my mind.

"Where are you going, soldier?" His name was Jac. I knew, because many of the other female soldiers flirted with him.

"To the track, sir."

"I've seen you running and riding your bike. Would you like to ride with me sometime?"

No. "Umm, yeah. Maybe. I mean, my schedule really doesn't have any openings as you can see."

"I do see. You'd better ask for a release next time."

I nodded and slid back under the fence. A week later, he presented me with a two-hour release so we could go for a ride. I tried to protest, but he had borrowed a high-end (at least compared to mine) road bike for me to ride, and I couldn't resist. The bike was light and smooth, and Jac talked to me about wheels and gears and cadence. It was magical, riding along the ocean. And before we got back to the base, I was in love. With the bike. Not the boy.

But I really liked the boy. He loved endurance sports, and was serious and reserved, just like me. We started training together and going to cafes, and for the first time ever, I felt a close connection. We were both so busy we hardly saw each other and I couldn't say that I was in love, but it was nice to have someone, another person to spend time with and care about. After a few months of training, I became a Madaseet (fitness instructor) and reported to my new work duty.

Shahar, my direct commander, stood about 6'1" and probably weighed over 250 pounds. He seemed even larger, however, with incredibly broad shoulders and bowed arms that never touched his sides. He had helped develop the modern-style of Krav Maga from a Yugoslavian military technique, and was now charged with teaching it to Israeli military personnel. He trained us, and we trained the troops. Shahar's seemingly choreographed movements and orders instilled respect and even fear in the troops passing through our base.

I mercilessly trained recruits in Krav Maga and fitness all day, and took the same approach to training myself. At some primal level, I always felt the need to be fitter—get faster, recover quicker. I ran on the track and rode my bike whenever I could squeeze it in. My commanders were sick of getting release requests from me just to go ride my bike. But I hadn't seriously considered myself a duathlete (a running and cycling athlete) until the morning Shahar told me I was.

My Saturday morning guard shift started late—after 7:00 a.m. I met Shahar at the front gate to get my assignment. I planned to beg for two hours off so I could get in a ride.

"You're racing in a duathlon today." Always serious. Always to the point.

"In a what?" He had mentioned that a few officers from other bases had been training for a duathlon near Wingate, but I never expressed an interest in doing it.

"It's a short one, so you'll be fine. Go get your bike, helmet, and running clothes." Shahar's words always dripped from his mouth, as if talking slowly would get his message in deeper. And his eyes hung on to yours for an extra uncomfortable moment after an order—just to make sure you really got it.

I thought about my clunky MBK bike, built more for commuting than racing. On my soldier's salary, I couldn't afford more. Plus, I just liked to ride. I was not a duathlete.

"I'm not really ready for a race," my mind thinking of an excuse to get out of it.

"You spend so much time training—let's go see what you've got." His eyes were serious, and slightly irritated. I turned and walked quickly back to my room.

He gives me two hours' notice to go do a race? How can I possibly be prepared? I don't know anything about this sport! My mind raced as I threw a water bottle, shorts, and my helmet into a military bag. *I don't even know the rules! Does the race start on foot or on the bike?*

Shahar parked on the road in front of my barracks. He had borrowed a base jeep with no top on it. He jumped out and threw in my bike. I cringed as the left pedal slammed into the bottom of the vehicle. I had always put a blanket down before loading my bike in a car, even though it was barely worth $300. I managed one last-ditch effort to persuade him that I wasn't ready.

"I don't know the rules—or the route. I'll probably get disqualified."

"Get in."

We drove in silence, the highway deserted. For the religious, Shabbat is a true day of rest. From Friday at sundown (as soon as there are three stars in the sky) until Saturday evening (twenty-five hours later), devout Jews don't do any work. As with any religion, people follow these rules to varying degrees. The most devout do not cook food, clean anything, open doors, rip toilet paper, or even flip a light switch during those hours. Needless to say, very few athletes in Israel could be considered religious. Shabbat is the best time to train, as everyone has time off work and the roads are deserted. Just like today.

A couple hundred people milled around the starting line, nothing but desert on all sides. I searched the crowd for my female competitors, and didn't see one. Shahar figured out how to register me and pinned a number on my chest. Other athletes jogged past, as I warmed up the only way I knew—boxing. Shahar held his hands up while

I threw punches and high kicks. I saw a young guy next to me checking the pressure on his tires. I didn't even own a floor pump, let alone have the basic knowledge about bike tire psi.

Not many people competed in running or riding back then, although the few who did seemed to be serious about their sport. Most wore proper bike shorts, shoes, and helmets. My bike couldn't compare to the Treks and Pinarellos hanging on the transition racks. Their racing bars and clip-in pedals seemed to taunt my cement-truck ride with its soft, big tires and regular flat pedals. While I warmed up like Rocky in my gym shorts, I had to wonder if everyone around me was quietly laughing.

The narrow starting line was crammed with about 150 athletes—all men, except for a handful of women. *I have to beat them.* The race started and finished with a 5 km run, with a 30 km bike ride in the middle. I thought I could run faster than I could bike, so I tried to push myself close to the front of the pack. I asked a few guys around me about how to transition to the bike, and any rules I should know.

"Stay off your bike in the transition area. Don't ride behind another athlete." That was it. My ten-second duathlon training seminar was over. Shahar, one of the few spectators, leaned over the edge and yelled at me.

"Hurry and finish! We have to get back to the base," his tone harsh with expectation. There were other soldiers competing, and he wanted proof that our style of training or our base in general was superior. Plus, I requested passes to train so often, I think he wanted me to prove they were worth it. I edged over to him for any final tips.

"You have mental strength." Pause with searing eye contact. "You train hard." Wait for it. "You need to win." His eyes burned into my head. What else could I do?

In the military, soldiers run at one speed—all of us together, long and steady. I did some sprint work on my own, but really had no idea how to pace myself at all. A group of men broke out at a very fast pace, and I settled in with a secondary group, keeping the leaders in sight. My body was used to carrying a 50-pound backpack, weapons, and heavy boots. Without the extra weight, I felt like a bullet. I could have gone faster, but decided to try and conserve on the first run, hang with these guys on the bike, and then see if I could kick it into another gear on the final leg.

I ran into the transition area as the leaders were whizzing by onto the bike course. I grabbed my bike and started running toward the zone where I could start pedaling. I quickly realized that the group of men I came in with was not with me. I turned my head, afraid that I had gone the wrong way. But instead, saw all of the others putting on their special bike shoes. Even in those days, serious cyclists used clip-in shoes, allowing them to actually push and pull on the pedals. I knew a few people who had them, but wasn't clear just how much they helped.

Later, as my cycling career progressed, I wouldn't dream of riding a bike without them. At the moment, however, I was just happy to have a quick transition. Shahar stood menacingly at the transition exit gate, his arms folded and head high. His head didn't move, just his eyes darted side to side as if collecting data for future review. I didn't make eye contact, jumped on my big black bike, and pushed alone out onto the bike course. My MBK was a tank, I wore running shoes on metal pedals, and I still made a conscience choice not to let anyone pass me. And they didn't.

I actually managed to pass five or six men (I never saw another female competitor after the starting line) and brought the lead group into view. *Who needs fancy clip-in shoes?* I maintained that position throughout the second run, and finished somewhere in the top ten. My pride and excitement stayed all on the inside, as Shahar never showed nor responded to emotions. He threw my bike back in the jeep and spun the steering wheel toward the road. As the tires hit the pavement, Shahar said, "You have to run faster."

"You're going so fast!"

The RAAM media crew finally caught up with us and pulled their van alongside me. A man with a microphone and video camera hung out the window.

"Hey, Leah! We've been trying to catch up with you all day! You're flying—you must be feeling great."

"I do," I yelled, turning my head to the left. As I did, a sharp jolt of pain shot down my neck. My eyes flew open in shock, and I turned my head back to the road. I finished the interview without looking at them, while quietly panicking.

"Looks like you're having trouble turning your head," he observed, implying something I didn't want to consider.

"No, I'm fine," I smiled. "Just keeping my eyes on the road! Safety first, right?"

He laughed. "Yeah, that's right. Well, keep up the great race! We'll see you in a few days!"

They sped ahead to rendezvous with our RV. I was sure they'd ask my crew about my neck. *It's not that bad.* I eased off the brake and sailed down the steep descents toward the prairies.

Kansas

"You're gonna catch a cold from the ice inside your soul."

Christina Perri

"Sorry, Leah, you have to stop for a second," Janessa yelled out the window.

My neck throbbed and shot pain down my spine and up into my head. The first few days of the race, I would have been annoyed to stop, while now I gladly unclipped and rested my forehead on my handlebars. *I wonder if a cheap Styrofoam® helmet would still be legal? It would feel a hell of a lot lighter.*

Sean ran up beside me and grabbed the bike. I didn't realize that I was slowly tipping over. I took the drink he offered and stood up.

"What's going on?" I asked. "Are we lost?"

"No, stalker official is giving us a penalty. She saw you roll through that stop sign back there."

RAAM officials prowl the entire course, watching for safety issues, lapses in protocol, and outright cheating. All of those things happen, and over a 3,000-mile course, I can't believe anyone could make it across without at least one minor infraction. Cyclists are allowed to make a "standing stop," meaning you don't have to unclip from your pedal at a stop sign, but you must slow down enough to be able to see your spokes going around.

I had rolled too quickly through the last one, and it wasn't because I had meant to. I hadn't even seen the sign.

"Shit." I didn't even have the energy to curse loudly. "You guys are going to have to call out everything on the radio. I can't see anything but a white line."

"Yeah, for sure. We got you, Leah."

Sean held the bike steady as I pushed back out onto the endless flat country roads, and my thoughts returned to Jac.

"Move in with me, Leah," Jac said. "We can save money if we get a place together." I had to admit, it did make sense.

He always spent Shabbat with his family and I'd go to my apartment in Herzliya Pituah, a ritzy district north of Tel Aviv. My dad had found it for me, and paid for it, but I didn't tell Jac that. He believed that I was paying for it on my meager soldier's wage. The truth was I'd asked my father to help me find a place. I had needed a place of my own, away from the base and away from my family, just to unwind. My Aunt Udit's house had been my one-night per week Shabbat home throughout basic training, and while I was grateful for the bedroom, the house rules had started to wear me out.

My Uncle Eli, a strict Orthodox Jew, followed the Saturday rules to the letter. No cooking, no shopping, no driving, no ripping toilet paper. The house actually had a built-in timer that disabled the electricity on Friday evening and started it back up Saturday evening. Eli explained that the twenty-four hours of no luxury was a visible commitment to God. The suffering proved your devotion. I loved my family, and really appreciated the room they offered, but sitting in the dark on my only day off from the oppressive military regime was irritating.

"Yeah, I guess we could," I answered hesitantly. I only had one night per week off the base. My mind started to race. *If we move in together, then he'll assume that I love him. And I'll have to LIVE with him. We are both too hardheaded. We will drive each other crazy.*

I shut it out of my mind. I'd already explained to Jac that I liked my space. So did he. I also explained that I wanted to take things slow—I was in no rush to become someone's wife, picturing myself cooking and changing diapers. He agreed. He was in no hurry either. But from the beginning, I knew he loved me more than I loved him. He wanted to marry me. He would pull me into a hug and put his cheek against mine, willing me to soften and hug him back. But I could only half hug him. My body would stiffen, the closeness giving me anxiety instead of the serenity I thought it should.

On most Friday nights, our one night together in our tiny house, I'd lie next to him and wonder why I continued to stay distant. The hot, sticky air would press down on me, willing me to sleep. I'd doze a few hours at most, and then rise onto the cool floor to pace and think. I heard a rabbi speaking on TV once who said sometimes it just takes time to fall in love with your partner and I felt so relieved. *Maybe I just need time.*

Our concrete bedroom had one small window on the wall next to the bed, but it was too high to look out. I'd take ten steps down the long way, stepping over the extension cord and ten steps back. Our tiny television with two crappy channels sat on a little table opposite the bed and I touched it each time I turned to go back the other way. *What is wrong with me? Why can't I just trust him? Talk about a life together? Would that be so terrible?* The heat would sometimes overwhelm me and I'd switch on the fan. Silently, I'd slide back down onto the bed and check my watch. *Just a little longer. Then I can go back to the base.*

I called that room "The Dungeon." It had concrete walls, floor, and ceiling, all gray, and barely any light. The raised platform held a foam mattress and our four duffel bags of clothes lined one wall. The lamp, with its extension cord snaking all the way into the kitchen, was too weak to even read by. But at least it pushed back the darkness. The light stayed on all night—I just couldn't bear the blackness. The room had no furniture or color or pictures. And believe it or not, I liked it that way.

When out training soldiers, I often went without a bed or toilet. A pillow was out of the question. I assumed if my home was actually comfortable, then going back to the tough conditions at the base would become unbearable. I'd seen it happen. Soldiers break down from the relentless grind of a gray military existence. I had to protect myself from comforts; get tougher.

I defined myself as a fighter and a soldier. But now I was a girlfriend. I had excelled at the first two; the latter never quite fit. But I pushed myself forward. *Everyone else can do this. Why can't I?* In the long, gray room, I battled with myself. The nightly guilt would invade, and I paced the concrete floor. *Ten steps down and ten steps back.*

As my military service came to an end, I started receiving notices for mandatory "testing." A date, time, and location were included in the letter, but nothing else. I'd show up, usually at a vacant apartment with one desk, two chairs, and one nondescript person with a folder. They would never identify themselves, just ask me to take a seat, and pull out their papers. I took a variety of psychometric tests.

"Place your pencil at the top of the page and close your eyes."

I obeyed.

"Draw a circle."

Done.

"Write the rest of this sentence. 'My mother says ... '; 'I fear that ... '; 'The dog seems ... '"; and so on.

Some tests resembled school—and I started to fear that my answers wouldn't be what they were looking for. I was positive that the Mossad was testing me; recruiting me. My excitement clouded my better judgment, and I called our mysterious family friend, Gil. His involvement with the Mossad was an assumption on my part, but his elusive comments and long absences made it obvious to all of us. High-level security personnel never reveal their positions or work. Anyone claiming to be an Israeli secret agent almost certainly isn't.

I knew all this, but I still called Gil and begged him to meet with me. I wanted him to verify my suspicions, to give me pointers on how to get through these tests and, regrettably, hoped he would welcome me to the club. He agreed to meet me on a street bench outside a large outdoor market. I arrived predictably early, and sat in the drizzling rain straining my eyes for his face. I hadn't seen him in years.

Exactly on time, he lowered himself onto the bench beside me.

"How are you?" he asked, not looking directly at me.

"I'm good. I'm almost finished at Wingate," I returned, and then spilled into a two-minute ramble about the letters and strange tests and what it all meant. It was the most I'd ever spoken to him in my life. His face didn't change and I abruptly stopped, realizing he wasn't really responding at all. I turned my eyes back to the street.

"This meeting should never have happened," he said, almost sympathetically.

My body went cold. I watched the drops falling into puddles and tried to keep my face stoic and straight. He sat beside me for another minute, his presence meant to soften the blow perhaps, and without a word, he rose and walked back into the crowd. I couldn't move. My eyes darted side to side, as I tried to absorb what had just happened. I had blown it. *Everything is a secret.* All that planning and work and sacrifice; it was all in vain. I sat in the rain letting the water run down my nose and my feet get soaked. It was the worst day of my life. *What am I going to do now?*

Other mistakes could be corrected with an apology, or a promise never to do it again. But not this. They don't give second chances to anyone. It felt like a death—sudden and permanent. There was nothing for me to do except grieve and move on. I walked back into the house, where Jac gaped at my soaked clothes and hair. I hadn't told him or anyone else about the letters. It's just not done. Everything is a secret. *Then why call Gil? So stupid.*

"Where did you go?" he asked.

"Nowhere."

The memory of that day sent a chill down my spine, and I shifted uncomfortably on my bike seat. The wind howled through the vents in my helmet, tugging at my bike, and drilling sand into my cheek. I'd been battling a nighttime crosswind for about ten hours, a stark change to the previous eight hours of tailwind where I'd zipped along at over twenty-five miles an hour.

"Well, this sucks," Connie quipped.

I barely had the neck strength to nod. *Yeah, it does.* My fingers and wrists ached from the effort of controlling the bike, as each blast of wind threatened to toss me in the ditch. I didn't dare let go of the handlebars to stretch them though.

"How much longer before we turn?" I asked, hoping to get the wind back in my favor again.

"Well ... it's Kansas. Not a lot of turning happening here."

I was afraid of that.

"There's a new course starting in the spring—Shooreem Oleem Hadasheem." Jac knew I was looking for a post-military plan, and since I hadn't told him about my Mossad dream, he thought this might be a good fit.

He explained that the four-month course would train personnel to deal with the new influx of domestic assault, drug trafficking, mafia, and homicide. A decade earlier, these crimes were rare, isolated events, but with a huge Russian and African immigration, the police were suddenly under-prepared. The Israel Police Force, trained and efficient at dealing with terrorism, couldn't keep up with the new shipments of cocaine and child shoplifters.

A week later, I drove to Tel Aviv to register. I walked up to the registration desk and asked for the forms. The teenage-looking clerk slowly raised his head.

"Sorry, what course are you interested in?"

"Shooreem Oleem Hadasheem."

"Oh, your husband has to come and register in person." His eyes returned to his huge stack of papers.

"Um, no. *I* want to register."

His eyebrows rose. "The course is only open to men—it was listed as a requirement on the posting."

I can read. "I know, but I'd still like to apply."

He mumbled something about not having the authority, and dropped his head again. I thought I might get turned down, but I thought I'd at least get to apply. I walked out with my fists clenched, already preparing to fight. This course could potentially redeem my chances with the Mossad. I might not become an international agent, but perhaps I could work my way up the police force into the Shabak (military intelligence), the Israel Security Agency (ISA), or another high-clearance position.

I called every high-ranking official I knew and made Jac do the same. I sent letters and spoke to my Wingate commanders about speaking out on my behalf. After a month-long fight with no end in sight, I finished my time at Wingate and moved into our tiny house full time. I trained more than ever, even winning the National Championship Duathlon. I waited and trained. My restlessness overtook me and I convinced Jac to ride the full length of Israel, both of us breaking the unofficial record.

Within a week after our bike ride, the Gulf War broke

out. The Canadian consulate called, offering me a quick one-way ticket out of there, and I was surprised. It hadn't even occurred to me that I could leave. When the warning sirens would wail, our Doberman, Ben, would sprint ahead of me into our improvised bathroom shelter. I'd pull on my government-issued gas mask and tape the doors while Ben lay at my feet, his head whipping back and forth trying to face the danger. Jac had gotten the dog for "us," but he quickly turned into my responsibility since Jac still worked full time at the base.

One day, the sirens went off while Jac was out for a run and he had a forty-minute run back to our house. He sprinted south along the highway, and a little white dog fell in right behind him. Far off explosions shook the ground while man and dog ran for their lives. With only a few kilometers left, the dog collapsed in the dirt, whimpering and exhausted. Jac tucked her under his arm and staggered the rest of the way home.

We spent the next few hours sweating in the sealed bathroom. I wore my gas mask, but Jac had long ago stopped believing those would actually save us. The white, matted dog lay splayed out beside me, trying to cool her body on the cement floor. I ran my hand along her swollen belly. *Great. She's pregnant.*

"Why can't we just go to Canada?" Jac suddenly shouted, wiping sweat from his forehead. "There is nothing for us here!"

He'd mentioned leaving Israel before, but I never thought he was serious. He knew I wasn't going anywhere. But the war was pushing him over the edge.

"If I wanted a life in Canada, I would've stayed there," I replied.

I had left North America to fulfill my dream: the military,

undercover work, the Mossad. I really liked Jac, or maybe I just liked the idea of him; of having someone care about me and walk the beach with me. But I had no intentions of changing my life plan for him. He wanted to leave his prestigious military post as a Lieutenant, training elite soldiers and IDF personnel, and find a career that paid more. And he'd decided Canada was the place to do it.

"I'm going," he said.

"Whatever."

We didn't talk about it again.

The war ended quickly, and we returned to our strained "normal." I started trying to find homes for the new dog's puppies, even though they weren't yet weaned. I named her "Poochki," a Russian slang term for "cutie pie" and the name seemed to fit, although she continued to be sickly and weak. One morning, I was riding my bike indoors on a stationary trainer, both dogs sitting close enjoying the breeze from my wheel. The platform supports the rear wheel allowing the tire to spin on a metal drum. The Israeli rush hour, full of honking and swerving cars, had scared me into riding indoors during certain hours. I churned my legs, watching my heart rate respond to the effort, when I heard a ringing sound. Jac, seated at the kitchen table, and I looked at each other. The foreign sound took us a moment to recognize—it was our phone.

Jac answered it and plugged his other ear to block the hum of the trainer, which he knew I wouldn't get off. He quickly turned to me and covered the mouthpiece.

"Leah—you have to take this."

No one had my phone number—not even my parents.

"What? No, tell them to call back later," I replied.

He stepped closer. "Leah, you must."

My heart sank. Perhaps something had happened to my mother. I grabbed the receiver, my hand slippery with sweat. "Yes?"

"This is Jacov Turner's office. You will report to Police Headquarters in Haifa in thirty minutes. Do you understand?"

"Y- Yes."

Turner was the Chief of Police, which in Israel is a position nearly equivalent to a President or Prime Minister. I quickly changed my clothes and drove to his office, gripping the steering wheel much too tightly. An assistant led me into a boardroom with a long mahogany table and eight chairs. Turner sat at the far end, the table coming up to his chest. He was tiny—a *lillipoot*, as we would say in Hebrew.

"So you're the troublemaker?" he began, motioning for me to sit at the other end.

"I don't want to be trouble. I just want to do this course, plus I'm overqualified for it, and I have no doubt that I can graduate. Why should it matter that I'm a woman?"

He tipped his head to one side, trying to read my seriousness.

"Okay. Listen. I can get you in, but you must know that many people don't want you there. Once you start, I can't help you."

"I understand."

He might have caved from public pressure, as several newspapers had recently run stories on my situation. I didn't know how the story had gotten out, but when reporters started calling me for statements, I gladly told them what I thought. I couldn't believe that women would be treated like this in Israel, a country I thought to be so modern and diplomatic. I didn't care how I'd finally been accepted. I walked out of his office with a renewed sense of purpose and hope.

Three weeks later, Jac and I drove up to the course base, the front gates surrounded by media crews. *I can't believe the course is THAT big a deal.* And then slowly it dawned on me. *They are here to see me.* I stepped out of the car into microphones and cameras, with shouts of "Are you a feminist?" and "Are you doing this for attention?" I walked straight ahead and kept my thoughts to myself. *If I wanted attention, don't ya think running naked through Jerusalem would be a lot easier?*

As the recruits gathered into lines, my new commander walked straight at me, stopping an inch from my ear.

"I see one tear come out of your eye, and you're done here. We understand each other?"

"Yes, sir."

Yep, he really had it in for me. The first week I lived in a tool shed—baking in the day and freezing at night. Other officers complained on my behalf and I was moved into a women's barracks with female officers stationed there for various other training. For four months, my commander gave me every crap duty, extra physical training, and cleaning detail he could think of. It was hell. Sometimes I thought I might crack, and I'd use my one phone call per week to talk to Jac. He had moved on from the military, but he understood harsh training and always knew exactly what to say.

Still, when I'd get a twenty-four hour pass, I'd ask Jac to bring my bike. He'd drive to the base, hand me my cycling gear, and I'd hand him my bag of clothes. Instead of riding home with him so we'd have more time together, I'd ride my bike for three hours or more before meeting him at home. His irritation was obvious, but the long, hard rides decompressed me.

I'd rather ride my bike than make it home for dinner with Jac. He is so nice to me—why can't I love him as he loves me?

I survived my torturer, completed all my course work, and graduated top three in my class. My commander actually had the decency to congratulate me, and tell me that I had certainly proven him wrong, and all future courses would be open to women. I was glad, but had to admit that's not why I did it. I needed this training to shoot me back up the ranks—get me back on track to do some real security work. I wasn't sure where they would send me first, but I couldn't wait to start.

A few weeks later, my anticipation nearly overwhelmed me as I tore open the assignment letter from Police Headquarters. *I'm sure I'll be stationed in Tel Aviv. Or Jerusalem. With my background, and finishing so high in my class, I'm sure the big departments will want me.* But, no. I got sent to the armpit of Israel. *Hadera?*

Graduating top three in my class - yes, that's Captain "tool shed"

Jac had just shrugged when I told him, and called the dogs out for a walk. We'd hardly spoken since I got back, using as few words as possible to take care of two dogs, bills, and the house.

This is not going to get better on its own. What am I going to do? I just didn't have the courage to discuss our relationship right then. *Next week.*

I walked slowly up to the police station, my feet shuffling, delaying the inevitable. I had received my orders five days ago, and just like all orders in Israel, there's no such thing as refusal. Hadera, run down and depressing, sat squarely in the middle of several smaller, run down and depressing villages. Drug crimes dominated the slew of other petty misconducts, and in my mind, that sort of work was beneath me. Almost anyone could get into the police department at that time and be a "Blue." I had military, martial arts, and the special course, Oleem Hadasheem, all on my resume. I couldn't believe they would send me here. Maybe it was a punishment for the dreaded "Gil" incident.

I stopped just short of the doors and glanced around at the barbed wire that circled the compound. Chips of stucco lay in the dirt, having fallen from the aging building and been left to wither in the sun. *This looks like a mental institution.* The inside wasn't much better, with cracked, dirty floor tiles and cheap metal furniture. Four female administrative staff sat at desks busying themselves with typing, moving papers, and smoking. One of them stood and walked toward me, her cigarette held pinched between her first and middle fingers while the rest of her hand rested on her obviously pregnant belly.

I caught myself staring, dumbstruck at the smoke swirling around her stretched blue police shirt. She walked right past me, and pulled open a filing cabinet. I looked hopefully at the other three, and with typical Israeli customer service, they ignored me.

"Sleha?" I said. *Excuse me?*

The closest secretary turned her head and exhaled a cloud of smoke. "Ken?" *Yes?* Her deliberately clipped voice sent her message loud and clear: I'm irritated and busy.

"Hanee Leah Goldstein," I offered.

"Ah, Goldstein. Lamala," pointing her thumb upstairs. "First office." She turned back to her papers and took another drag from her cigarette. *Nice to meet you all too.*

I walked around the desks and slowly climbed the stairs. The hallway was lined with closed doors, except the first door on the right. I walked into the open office, and instantly felt the energy change from mental institution to total prickville. A dark-skinned man, slight and barely taller than me rose from behind the desk. His small dark eyes looked me up and down as he put his hands onto the desk and leaned closer to me.

"Before we start, go make me a cup of coffee." It was a command, not a request.

I froze. My skin went cold and a shiver went through my toes. The next two seconds felt like minutes, as the anxiety and pressures and disappointments of the past year crashed down on me. I had begged and fought and waited for this? The ensuing year flashed through my mind. *I make you coffee and then what? A neck massage? Mop your floor? No fucking way.*

"No," I stated firmly, raising my chin.

This man could make my life very difficult. My police work fate was in his hands. But I didn't care. I leaned forward back at him. I didn't care if he assigned me every night shift, cavity search, and shit detail there was. I wasn't going to start off my police life feeding his obviously inflated ego. Stunned, he stood up straight, trying to find words to fire back at me. His assistant, a man straightening the workstation right behind him, quickly interjected.

"Oh, I'll make the coffee. I've already started some, actually."

He walked out of the office, obviously already well versed in kissing the commander's butt, and I took a seat. Mr.

Coffee proceeded to lecture me about my training, two weeks with each department including narcotics, domestic issues, terrorism, investigative, traffic and street crimes, surveillance, and homicide. The only thing I wouldn't be expected to do was write any complex reports. Obviously, he'd heard about my poor Hebrew writing skills. Then he rattled on about long shifts, no special treatment, and the tough job our station faced due to the area. I wondered if Jac would mind my long hours. I wondered if he was still mad at me. And driving home that afternoon, I had to wonder if I even still had a relationship to go home to.

As soon as I opened the door, I knew the white dog was dead. I could smell it; the oppressive heat already starting to decay her body. Ben sat panting in the far corner of the kitchen and stared at his companion. I leaned in, and could see her body pressed up against the kitchen drawers. Yellowish fluid pooled all around her gaping mouth; her eyes were open and empty. A folded note sat in the middle of the kitchen table, Jac's neat printing on the front: *LEAH*.

"Jac?" My voice quivered slightly. I wasn't sure if I wanted to hear a reply or not. My heart beat in my ears as I strained to hear any sign of him. But he was gone.

I slammed the door behind me and Ben ran to hide in the bedroom. *Some watchdog.* I walked across the room and stood straight above the ball of matted fur.

"Poochki," I whispered and slid down onto the floor beside her. "He's gone, isn't he?" I said aloud, to no one. I read his note, which explained that he'd gone to Canada, and that he hoped I'd join him. I glanced over at the dogs' full food bowls. He'd fed them this morning and left. We both knew I wouldn't follow him. It was over. After practically driving him away with my coldness and anger, I was still shocked that he'd actually left me. Something iced over in me that day, something that I wasn't sure I'd ever be able to thaw.

There's no such thing as love.

Is there love? True love? It seems like a dream. Am I in a dream?

"Leah!" The megaphone squealed. I jerked my head up, and pain shot through my neck like an electric shock. My hand shot up to cup my chin as I whimpered. I knew I was falling asleep again. The crew had warned me that they'd be using the megaphone and car horn if necessary. *Must have been necessary.*

I pushed my call button. "I need more Aleve."

"Nope," came the reply. "You have to wait one more hour, and then you can have Tylenol."

I let my head drop again. I forgot that we'd resorted to alternating pain medications, "piggybacking" them so I could take more and hopefully not end up with an ulcer. The pain-relief tag team dulled the throbbing ache, but didn't come close to relieving it. I'd developed Shermer's Neck, named after the first RAAM racer to get it, Michael Shermer. The condition mostly strikes men, and mostly after eight or nine days into the race. Mine started within the first four.

When we stopped for a break that night, I sat on the edge of my motel bed while my mother helped me take off my jersey. I could feel Connie and Lori staring at my back, and I could sense their anxiety and doubt. I knew they were whispering about my safety, and wondering if it might just be better to pull out. My temples throbbed, and my chin sat almost comically on my chest, but the idea of quitting

Police Academy

couldn't have been farther from my mind. I had to reassure them.

"Well, I guess I'm just going to have to finish like this," I offered, as cheerfully as I could manage.

"Leah, are you sure? You can barely see ahead of you," Lori said quietly.

"I've never quit a race in my life."

Connie, a seasoned athlete with crazy tendencies like mine, immediately switched to proactive. "Then we need to come up with something to hold your neck up. Simple as that."

I fell back onto the pillow, dreading the pain that would come ninety minutes from now when I'd have to get back on that damn bike. Meanwhile, my crew called an emergency meeting and started brainstorming ideas for my fallen head. We'd already tried two types of neck braces. The soft one didn't do enough to matter, and the hard one made it impossible to breathe. I had ditched them both within minutes.

I quickly fell asleep, with visions of Aleve pills dancing in my head.

Missouri

"Leah, we have to shave your head."

"Not gonna happen!"

Janessa and I bantered back and forth as Ed drove us to our nightly pit stop motel. They had put a strip of duct tape on the pavement, marking the spot where I'd stopped. After my few hours of sleep, they would place my bike back on that line, ensuring I hadn't missed even one inch of the route.

"Leah, we have an idea to use kinesiology tape on your neck, but I think it will work better if we can attach it farther up on your head."

Connie had brought along some of the tape, a stretchy, sticky athletic tape used to support injured joints. She'd used it on herself and on some of the athletes she'd coached, with fairly good success. Janessa thought it was a great idea and Lori, a kinesiologist, thought it would work even better with a half-shaved head.

"Think of something else," I muttered. I was cranky and nauseous from the pain. Ed walked me into my room, holding my arm like I was a hundred years old. I could no longer balance myself off the bike, kind of like sea legs. I had bike legs.

I took a quick shower, keeping one hand on the wall at all times, and pulled on a clean t-shirt and shorts. The best Egyptian sheets couldn't have felt better. I held onto the doorframe as I shuffled back into the room. Janessa, Connie, and Lori stood side by side with scissors, razors, and tape in their hands.

"We gotta do it, Leah," Janessa stated apologetically.

Outnumbered and too exhausted to argue, I slowly lowered myself facedown onto the bed.

"Whatever," I mumbled into the flat pillow.

I drifted in and out of consciousness, while they cut off my hair from the top of my ears down. Then they treated me to a barber-inspired shave, complete with warm towel. They sprayed Tough Skin, an adhesive, on my neck and back, and pressed the strips of tape from just behind my ears down to my mid-back.

"Are you finished?" I whined. The position killed my neck, and gratefully I rolled onto my side. I could feel the support from the tape instantly, and was glad they had talked me into it. It was only hair. As I drifted off to sleep, I could hear them critiquing their handiwork.

"Do you think it's enough?"

"Yeah. It's going to hurt like hell taking it off."

"It looks like four pink octopi fighting over her hair." Laughter.

"What's left of it." More laughter. "And who in the hell says 'octopi'?"

I worked with the regular "blue" police for only a few weeks, when I discovered that the Belush also operated out of our station. The Belush, an undercover unit, dealt with drugs, terrorism, murder, and domestic assault, all the headline-stealing crimes. Of course, I wanted to progress in my career, but was shocked when after only a few months I was called into the director's office. The Belush wanted me.

"So, Leah, we'd like to send you right away for training.

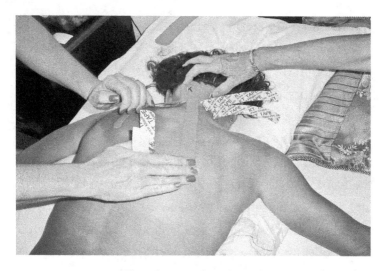

Shaved, sprayed, and taped

We don't have any women in our department right now and I think you'd be a perfect fit," he stated directly. He wasn't asking me; it was an order. But he had an easy smile and sparkly brown eyes that made it easy to reply.

"Yes, sir. I'd be honored."

He reminded me of Bosley from Charlie's Angels, with his sleek brown hair and sport coat. I headed off to advanced Belush training smiling to myself. *I work for Bosley!*

The course, however, seemed rushed and too general. Two weeks later, I was already sliding into a squad car to start my on-the-job training. I shifted uncomfortably in the backseat, my jeans sticky in the oppressive heat, my thoughts racing. *Do not screw this up. If someone captures me, always claim to know nothing. If you think someone is strapped with a bomb, don't approach and call for back up.* I rolled situations around in my head like dress rehearsals.

I wondered if my meager Belush training had actually prepared me for the next level of crime. While I felt relieved
to be free of Mr. Coffee and the daily drudgery of the uni-
formed police officers, I was also scared as hell that I just
wasn't prepared for this.

The sun was almost directly overhead as my "instruc-
tors," Rami and "Trident," the gum chewer, jumped into
the front seat. The guys all told me he chewed non-stop,
and they were right. I could never remember his real
name, so I always called him Trident. I actually became
his supplier after a few months, having my mother ship me
boxes of Blue Menthol Trident. I chewed gum constantly
too. I think it was mostly our way of dispensing some of
the tension. We all found our little ways of diverting our
minds away from the work we were doing, and gum chew-
ing was the drug of choice for Trident and me.

That first day, he chomped away on his less-flavorful
Israeli gum as he drove Rami and me around Or Akeva,
a small village on the outskirts of Hadera. It was my first
day, and I was just supposed to watch and learn. Learn
the town and the important places. Learn which crimes
mattered and which didn't. Learn when to follow the book
and when to throw it out.

The police station radio squealed with calls and alerts,
but I could barely hear it. The built-in radio blared rock
music and drowned out the scanner and their voices. I
shouted above the noise, "I thought we were supposed to
be listening to all police calls?" Trident looked over his
right shoulder and half-grinned at me. "You will learn to

listen to three things at once, newbie. This is part of your training." I strained to hear everyone's voices. Suddenly, Rami slapped off the radio and turned up the scanner.

A known international drug dealer had been spotted nearby. The Belush had been tracking him for months and had records of him trafficking heavy drugs from Lebanon and Egypt into Elat, the southernmost Israeli city, wedged on a sliver of land between Egypt and Jordan. I had heard this criminal's name several times before, and judging by the looks on the guys' faces, they had too. He would be a huge bust for us, and here he was in our own backyard.

Trident whipped the car around. "This is going to be an exciting day for you, Leah—we've been after this guy for years." We all kept our hands on the door handles as we sped through the streets, standard procedure for Israeli Police. We were actually taught how to open a car door and jump out running while the car was still moving. My first night on the job, and I was going to have remember all my training.

"What does this guy look like?" I yelled over the seat.

"Are your shoes tied tight?" he shot back.

I glanced down at my bright white Nikes. "Yeah. But you still haven't told me what this guy looks like!"

He mumbled, "Dark hair, kind of tall, brown eyes!" *Awesome, that's the whole damn country!* The guys' eyes bulged out of their heads, focusing on the job ahead.

I got no more instructions as we drove slowly up to a small group of people in a vacant lot. At first, our plain white Ford Escort drew no attention and I had a few seconds to scan the crowd. My eyes immediately focused in on two men, standing with their backs to us. A small, scrawny guy rested his elbow up on a broad, brawny shoulder and, as the car rolled closer, he took a quick glance back. His eyes narrowed. He knew it was us.

Although the Belush rode in unmarked cars, it was always unmarked white Ford Escorts, and there was no element of surprise with seasoned criminals. The little man nudged his friend and the broad shoulders turned to reveal an equally large chest and arms. His eyes widened, and in an instant, he bolted down an alley. *That's him.* Rami and I jumped out of the car and Trident called for backup. "Leah—you go around that way!" Rami shouted, giving no indication of which way he actually wanted me to go.

Rami ran straight into the scattering crowd, and I sprinted after Mr. Muscles by myself.

I was a fast runner and kept him in my sight across a playground and toward an old warehouse. *I am alone. Totally alone. First night. All alone.* I felt something hard bump my leg, and thought maybe someone had thrown a bottle at me. As I came around the corner of the building, he glanced back at me. His sleeveless t-shirt was dark with sweat, his chest heaving with indignation. No way was he going quietly. We locked eyes and in a split second he spun and sprinted down an alley. I was certain that was our guy, and had no choice but to chase him. *What exactly am I going to do if I catch up to him? He's as high as a kite—it may take a bullet to stop him. Am I really going to shoot someone on my first night?*

My heart was pumping uncontrollably—and not from fatigue. This man was actually quite big, by Israeli standards—probably 6'3" and close to 220 pounds. Rami had underestimated him, and I was glad. If I had known his actual build, I might have hesitated to give chase. But here I was, running after an international drug dealer who just happened to be twice my size. He turned right into an abandoned six-story building and headed up the concrete stairs. I could hear his feet slamming into the stairs above me, and his breath growing heavier and heavier. *Or is that mine?* I felt my legs starting to slow, and I pulled on the metal banister on the corners to keep up. BAM, BAM, BAM! He pounded on a door at the top of the stairs. "Let me in! God dammit, open the door!" he screamed. I slowed slightly, came around the corner and we locked eyes again.

"Get your hands up! You're under arrest!" I yelled at him, sliding my hand down to my revolver. My hand pressed against my hip—and my whole body went cold. I slapped a few other pockets, just like in the movies. As if one would actually accidentally put their weapon in the wrong pocket! I didn't have it. I must have dropped my gun out in the crowd. His eyes lightened and a flicker of hope dashed across his face. He knew I was unarmed. The small knife holstered to my lower leg tempted me to pull it, but I knew a three-inch blade would simply enrage him further.

I could hear Rami and Trident downstairs yelling for me. Thirty seconds after jumping out of the car, they had realized that they shouldn't have let me go alone. They had chased the wrong guy before sprinting back to find me. I put my hands behind my back, as if I was pulling out another weapon. "I will shoot you. Turn around and get on the ground," I stated as calmly as I could. He didn't believe me for a second. He wiped spit from the corner of his mouth and grinned at me, his pupils so dilated that his eyes looked pure black. He launched himself off the top landing, sprinting back down the stairs.

I spun around and jumped four stairs down to the next level, and flew around the corner. I begged my legs to go faster as I took the stairs two at a time. My mind was racing. *He has a gun; he is high as a kite and can probably overpower me even if I disarm him. Shit, shit, shit!*

Just as my feet hit the last landing, Rami and Trident ran straight past me with guns drawn. I heard them both cock their weapons, and I braced for shots. My pursuer tripped down the last small flight of stairs and crashed onto the cement floor. He rolled onto his side and stared into my eyes, his sweaty chest heaving in time with mine. Rami walked straight at him, his gun aimed squarely at his nose. He ordered him onto his belly, and threw me his handcuffs. I yanked his thick wrists into the restraints. Feeling the first hints of elation, I squeezed them down even tighter. With a small smile, I looked up at the guys, fully expecting pride beaming from their faces.

But they were not proud. They were horrified. Trident tilted his head at me, pulling my gun out of the back of his pants.

"Lose something?" I looked at the ground. My gun had dropped in the playground, not ten feet from a merry-go-round. "What the hell, Leah! You know you could get a six-month suspension for this?"

It was a rhetorical question. Everyone knew that. I took my gun and slid it back into my holster and started the long walk back to the car.

After our guy was safely stowed in a police cruiser, we allowed ourselves to actually absorb what had just happened. Rami and Trident shook their heads at me and small smiles broke into nervous laughter as we recounted the incident.

"Well, it wasn't pretty, but we got him," said Rami, motioning to the car.

As we bounced back into our headquarters parking lot, my stomach started to roll. *Why didn't I keep my hand on my gun? We were taught that! What if they tell my commander that I actually dropped the damn thing? I'll be a laughing stock.*

Bosley met us in the lobby, his face bursting with elation.

"You got the son of a bitch!" He slapped Trident's shoulder and guided us all over to a bench. Two other Belush officers took our resigned perp into the interrogation room, while the rest of the station milled around, wanting to hear all the details of our huge bust.

"So—let's have it," smiled Bosley, leaning in to absorb every detail. Trident and Rami glanced at each other. I stared at the ground.

"Leah chased him down. All by herself," said Rami.

My head snapped up. I started to explain how the guys helped, and it was a team effort, but Bosley was so excited that he and the guys just talked over me. Bosley put his hand on my shoulder and firmly shook me. "I knew I made the right choice picking you!"

Across the lobby, Mr. Coffee gripped the edge of the copy machine, overhearing the entire exchange.

Bosley called over to him, "Hey, sergeant! Why don't you get our hero a cold glass of water?" Bosley knew nothing of our initial meeting, and, therefore, missed the joke when I followed up with, "No, sergeant, make that a coffee."

For weeks after the bust, I worried that Rami or Trident would meet privately with Bosley and tell him the truth. How could they not? I felt isolated as the only woman in the department, and wrongly assumed none of the men would want to work with me, especially if those two told everyone that I'd dropped my gun. The other officers had no choice but to work with me, of course, since we all rotated through shifts and squad cars. Everyone changed partners every single day.

Only a few days later, I was partnered with Yossi, a young, attractive officer reputed to flirt with the female staff. He followed me up the circling stairway, heading to the meeting room to get our daily briefing, and I felt his hand slide across my butt. I whipped around, pulling my Jericho out of its holster and pointed it at his face.

Bosley had insisted that I start off my Belush career with two oversized handguns on my hips—Jerichos. He'd also floated a rumor that I had killed seven people, hoping the local criminals would respect me out of fear. The guys in our unit all knew the truth though. I was just a small, female rookie in an all-male unit. I had to earn my own respect.

"What in the hell are you doing?" I shouted, my anger way past appropriate. "Would you do that if your wife was standing here?" He slowly shook his head. "If you wouldn't do it with her here, then why is it okay now?" I let the gun drop to my side; Yossi's eyes were still wide and incredulous. I softened. "Sorry," I mumbled, "I just can't stand that crap." Stunned, he offered a sincere apology and assured me it wouldn't be repeated. I believed him.

A few weeks passed, I gratefully traded my Jerichos for a much more reasonable Beretta handgun, and instead of shunning me, the guys embraced me. Rami improved my shooting, taking me out into the desert to fire at beer cans. Trident taught me to profile people by watching their hands when they talk, how they wear their hair, and the type of jewelry on their hands. I observed interrogations and learned the telltale signs of liars.

Being the only woman in our station also meant that I became an expert in cavity searches. If a drug suspect was arrested, a cavity search was mandatory on his or her companions. All females came to me. All matter of bodily fluids spattered my uniform on a nearly weekly basis and, as disturbing as that was, it was the safest part of my job.

During my first year with the Belush, as drug crime accelerated, terrorism seemed to grow more disturbing and closer to home. A police officer from a station not far from ours had been stripped naked, his genitals tied with a rope, and his body dragged behind a truck until his genitals ripped off. Another officer was hanged near an Arab village in the north. And even with security checks at every entrance, bombs still slid into buses and malls, including one woman with bombs strapped to her baby.

I felt some compassion. I knew all about the Israeli-Arab conflict and, although I was horrified at these crimes, I still felt peace was possible. I sincerely thought that if the IDF and police units did their job in protecting Israel, and the governments continued to broker treaties, these problems would fade over time. I felt important in doing my part of the peace process. But as time passed and my frustration grew, my compassion for humans in general seemed to wither. I grew harder, more skeptical, until eventually I could feel the hate start to grab hold of me—and there was nothing I could do to stop it .

Rami and I drove into the mountains near Haifa to check on a small police station. A small Arab village sprawled out just behind the building, and I could hear high-pitched chanting and hand clapping before Rami turned off the engine. We walked toward the door, the noise overpowering. "What's going on? Is there a wedding or something?" I asked the two officers who met us just inside. They looked at each other, then one asked Rami, "Does she really not know?" He shook his head, and they gently explained that a woman had been accused of adultery. She was being stoned to death.

"You're kidding!" I smiled. I searched their faces and quickly my disbelief turned into anger. "How can that be? This is a democratic country!" Silence. "Why don't you stop them?" I asked, shocked. "You see that line out there?" Rami pointed fifty feet away from the building. "This is Israel. That is not." *Humanity doesn't exist.* Interestingly, there is no mention of stoning adulterers in the Quran— but it's in the Torah AND the Bible. *Go figure.*

At the end of every shift, I felt depleted and hollow. The guys seemed to just shrug off the day as they removed their weapons and boots. I couldn't understand how these men could just go home to their wives and kids, and not take the job home with them. The peoples' voices echoed in my head as I pedaled the long flat highways. Like the hero-in-addicted mother who pleaded and screamed at me as I carried her baby out of her house, or the guy who begged for mercy after we picked him up for spousal abuse. We dragged him out into the desert, and I watched while my partner punched his face and kicked his stomach, yelling questions and insults. "Does this feel good to you? How's it feel to get beat by somebody tougher that you, huh?" Instead of feeling good for having stood up to an abused woman's husband, however, I just felt less human.

As I grew more confident with my weapon, partners, and protocols, Bosley sent me more and more on special assignments. Special task forces, made up of Belush, soldiers, and other agents routinely went into Arab villages looking for known terrorists. I rarely knew anything more than an address. Our mission was to get into the house and make an arrest. However, a household with an extremist position most certainly wouldn't easily open the front door to Israeli police.

So we, in our plain clothes, would approach the front door with fake tax documents and explain to the resident (almost always the woman of the house) that her husband owed taxes or something along those lines, and that's the only reason the police were on her doorstep. I'd explain to her that she would have to pay, or the "tax agents" would be forced to seize some of their personal items as payment. An Arab woman wouldn't be allowed to open the door to a man, so I was always the greeter. The Belush in position A.

Sometimes she'd refuse us entry, but usually, she'd allow me and up to four other officers into her living room. I kept her occupied asking questions about how long they had lived on this property and her husband's job, while the guys snooped around the house looking for chemicals, fuses, or any other bomb materials. In most cases the intrusion, which no doubt she'd be suspicious of, did not deter classic Middle Eastern hospitality.

"Would you like some coffee?" she'd ask, already preparing drinks, cookies, fruit, and nuts. There was no point in refusing. Middle Easterners simply must offer food to visitors, no matter how much they loathed them.

"Thank you," I'd say.

Most of the Arab women were lovely, and I'd pretend to take sips of the strong, sweet coffee while listening to stories about her fruit trees and beautiful kids. The contradiction was absurd. The women chatted with their sweets and hot drinks, while the men confiscated glassware and trinkets, maintaining the ruse. Many households had up to eight children, and I couldn't help but look into their eyes and wonder if we were just creating the next generation of terrorists.

I took my job very seriously, though, and had no doubt that we were making Israelis safer. If we take away a bomb, or arrest a potential carrier, then we've saved countless lives. We could never forget that there is a significant group of people who will never be satisfied while you draw breath, simply because of your birth. It's an indescribable feeling, to absorb that amount of hatred from another human being's eyes.

My first taste of how deep this hatred was happened on a trip into an Arab village, which started off like many others.

"Good morning, ma'am," I said calmly in Hebrew. "We are from the Israeli Police Department on behalf of the tax department. Is your husband at home?"

"No."

"Well, you see, he owes taxes from last year, so you'll have to pay that amount or we'll be forced to confiscate your personal property," I pointed at our phony tax papers. "May we come in?"

She swung open the door and I balked at her eagerness. It was too quick. Too sure. The guys shuffled forward, antsy to get on with it, so we walked into her living room. She pointed to the sparse furniture, and not wanting to appear rude, we sat. She pulled a key from her pocket, locked the front door deadbolt, and slipped it into her bra.

Why would she do that? Fight or flight?

She muttered something about coffee, turned into the kitchen, and I relaxed slightly. A little girl, maybe three years old, stood at my side staring up at me with enormous brown eyes. She was probably fascinated by my blonde hair, which was kept very blonde for those times when it was better to appear to be a tourist rather than an Israeli.

I gave her a small apologetic smile. *Sorry, we are looking for your dad. We will take him if we find him, but we'll probably just root through your house and take some teacups.* I started to smell natural gas and looked back up at her mother, who was now rummaging around in kitchen drawers. I could hear the multi-layered hissing of all four burners. None of them were lit, and I could not see a kettle. My body went numb.

"Allah Agba! I know why you're here! I am not afraid to die! What about you, huh? I know who you are!" she pulled a match out of the small box in her hand, and scraped the head across the side. "You can all die with me! Allah Agba!"

Like hell I am. "I'm outta here," I nearly whispered, praying that her matches were old. I took three running steps toward a large window, while pulling out my Beretta. I smashed the glass with the butt end and crashed through the frame with my body. The others spilled out right behind me. A commotion would attract a crowd, and a crowd meant we'd be in serious danger, so we race-walked back to our van, pretending to merely be in a hurry, not actually running for our lives. Our driver peeled away and didn't stop until we were back across the line.

I sat in the passenger seat and leaned my head against the window. My throat threatened to squeeze closed, so I distracted myself counting the scarce trees along the highway.

The silence enveloped us, all of us trapped in our own thoughts. I had to tell Bosley I couldn't do this anymore. I knew he was going to order psychological debriefing, a mandatory exercise to help us deal with the traumas of our job. I, still convinced that I was tougher than most, had always refused. The thought of sharing my feelings with a complete stranger felt more like trauma than jumping through a plate glass window.

After my twelve-hour day shift, Bosley came into the locker room. "Leah, Eli, and Schmoleck! You've got an hour off, then be back here at 9:00 p.m. wearing your blacks."

Night assignment. Great. We all kept a dark pair of pants and shirt in our locker for working at night; better to blend in.

Another officer, Rami, who somehow escaped the night shift this time, invited me over to grab some food and I gratefully accepted. His wife, Dahlia laid out at least fifteen plates of food. Roasted fish, stewed sweet potatoes with figs, fresh vegetables with chopped nana (mint), watermelon, fresh pita bread, and tahini filled the table and the air, and I suddenly missed my mother. I hadn't thought of her in weeks.

I forced down some fruit and bread, the heat and exhaustion dampening any hunger.

"Stay focused," Rami said under his breath, turning his head away from his three kids arguing at the other end of the table.

"What do you mean?" Night shift was brutal for most; but I could stay awake fairly easily, even when my body screamed for sleep. "I really don't mind the extra work."

His eyes got wider. "Make sure your weapons are fully loaded and you're stocked." That meant a full ammo belt with every allowable weapon—the works.

"Do you know something I don't?" My heart was accelerating.

"Just keep your eyes open, and don't drop your goddamn gun."

Rami's concern for me was comforting. He was probably the closest thing to a friend I had, and he didn't even know where I lived. His nervousness that night, however, was more than that. He was afraid. As I armed myself back at our station, I replayed his words in my head. *Stay focused.* Beretta, lower leg knife. *Fully loaded.* Bullet-proof, stab-proof vest. *Keep your eyes open.* Extra magazines, radio, earpiece. *Don't drop your goddamn gun.*

I watched Eli and Schmoleck pull on their boots in silence. They couldn't be more opposite, I thought. Eli, tall, lanky, and always pissed off had thick, short facial hair that made him look more like a porn star than a cop. And classy Schmoleck, short, serious, with a gray waxed moustache that curled up at the ends. He was so good at his job, I was convinced there wasn't a drug dealer around he couldn't squeeze information out of. I dreaded being paired with Eli, perpetually grumpy, practicing the art of "aggressive arrests" with extra shoves and punches when he felt like it.

"Ma anyaneem! Haeem at bamach zoar?" the other officers would yell at him. *What's the matter! Do you have your period?*

Soft-eyed Schmoleck, only one year from retirement, preferred to work alone. So even though I often hoped to partner with him, it had occurred only once.

During that one night shift with Schmoleck, we went back to the base for a two-hour nap. "Are you sure we're allowed to do this?" I'd asked.

"Cops are better when they're rested," he winked at me. "The world won't end tonight." As we lay down on floor mats, the radio next to our heads, he told me, "Leah, we will never be finished. Drugs will never end. Just like terrorism. We can only try to maintain it. Contain it. That is all. We can do no more."

I was starting to agree with him, as very few things we did felt satisfying. Arresting the same person six times for the same crime eroded the thrill.

Tonight, however, felt different. Electric. Schmoleck and I loaded the police car with M16s, flash grenades, tear gas, batons, and Uzis. *Make sure you're stocked.* The three of us drove north toward Haifa and pulled off near a highway rest area. An armed van, with barred windows and a supersized grill guard, slowly pulled up beside us. The van didn't stop. The passenger simply nodded at Schmoleck, and we followed.

We turned east, up into the mountains. Arab villages surrounded us, and I couldn't contain my curiosity any longer.

"Do you know what we're doing tonight?" I asked, turning to Schmoleck hopefully.

"It's a terrorist. That is all I know." I turned forward,

looking out at ever-narrowing roads. I chastised myself. *Don't ask questions. Just shut up. They will tell you what to do.* Asking too many questions is taboo in Israel; even more so in the Special Forces. The other men in the van could be from the military, or Yasam, a counter-terrorist unit, or even the Mossad. Agents from different branches of the Israeli Special Forces often completed special operations together. But they never, ever, asked questions.

The windy roads turned to dirt and the dust created a haze between our little car and the van. I started to worry we'd lose them, when suddenly the van turned into an empty lot, mostly hidden by the steep terrain. Schmoleck turned off the engine. Four men in varying combinations of camouflage and black clothing jumped out of the van while the driver motioned for us to get in. I slid the side door shut as the driver slowly pulled back on to the road. He turned his lights off and crept forward. I could barely make out the mountainside on our left into which this path, which could hardly be called a road, was carved. I assumed the other side was cliff, so I kept my eyes down. I wondered who could be this important to necessitate so many agents.

The man in the passenger seat turned to me and pointed at my hip.

"What in the hell is that?"

I glanced down; subconsciously making sure it was there. "It's a Beretta."

He pursed his lips. "We don't play with toys here. Take an Uzi. Make sure it's loaded and the safety is off."

The van was *loaded*. Sniper rifles, tear gas, grenades, riot gear, and of course, Uzis. On patrol with the Belush, I stowed a baby Uzi as my automatic gun (all agents were required to carry them in their vehicles), my small hand fit the stock better. I took the closest regular-sized Uzi and pulled the strap over my shoulder. I couldn't help but wonder why in the hell they picked me for this sort of assignment, but I hoped it was a test. Could the Mossad be watching me? I steeled myself, ready to do whatever was ordered.

The van turned into a driveway with stone walls on either side. Just enough light shone from the moon to reveal rows and rows of cars. There must have been a hundred, and all with Israeli plates. My mind raced. Car theft had been out of control in our area, with at least one reported every day. *Is that why we are here? For a king pin auto thief?* But by the way the agents in front looked at each other, I knew the car cemetery was merely a bonus. The driver put his hand to his mouth, indicating there would be no more talking. I slid my earpiece into my left ear and checked that my radio was on.

The van rolled to a stop near a large house, and we all quickly got out. We crept along a winding fence to an elaborate gate with hanging flowers and stone statues. The three front men stopped abruptly and put their heads together, a quick discussion ending with the driver ordering me back to the van. "Stay outside the vehicle," he whispered. "Keep your weapon engaged and eyes open. I will signal you with code word 'Tse Fa,' at which time you will get in the driver's seat and start the engine."

My spine stiffened. *"Viper" is our code word? I hate snakes.*

"Are you a driver?" He meant, of course, did I have experience driving on missions of this kind. I shook my head, wondering if passing traffic on the highway shoulder at 100 mph just to get home to my bike would count. *Doubt it.*

"Well, you are now. Anyone approaches before I radio you—shoot them." I nodded, and noticed two men behind him attaching silencers to their handguns.

I half jogged back to the van, as if our assault vehicle was my new partner and if I stood next to it, at least I wouldn't be alone. I crossed behind the back of the van, and peered around the front windshield, keeping the van between the house and me. The front door was slightly ajar, and the five men I'd approached it with were gone. I scanned the surroundings for the other four. Had they walked up to the house? Were they just covering us from a distance? I could see the end of my Uzi starting to vibrate. *Is that nerves? Or are my arms just fatiguing from this heavy damn gun?* After two minutes or ten, my radio crackled, "Tse Fe!"

I jumped into the van and turned the key. Within twenty seconds, all five men from the house quickly joined me, even Schmoleck looked agile. Driver guy, now sitting beside me, pointed his finger sharply forward, and I put the van in gear. They hadn't arrested anyone.

I weaved my way back down the mountain with no headlights, passenger guy's finger urging me to go faster. I could barely see the side of the single-track lane, with only blackness beyond. *How in the hell can I go faster? I* started praying to every higher power I'd ever heard of. *God? Jesus? Buddha? Can we all just come together and keep me from rolling us down a cliff? Please?* The fear of tumbling down the rocks with enough ammo to blow up Jerusalem, suddenly outweighed whatever just went down five minutes ago. Somehow, I kept us on the road and I gratefully skidded back into the vacant lot, the other personnel simultaneously appearing out of the trees. Eli, Schmoleck, and I slid back into our white Ford Escort, and without a word, it was over.

The atmosphere between Arabs and Jews started to shift that month, with bombings and retaliation strikes happening weekly. For the first time, female terrorists were striking malls and shopping centers, and security measures responded. Most crowded areas provided a security force to screen shoppers as they enter; they still do. Everywhere else in the world, security is tight leaving a store, but in Israel they get you on the way in. Previously, most women, regardless of religion, would barely be searched. Security guards might have checked a woman's bag, but rarely anything more.

But after several attacks, two security guards were required at every door, and body scanners used more often. Anyone deemed suspicious, most often an Arab, could be pulled aside for questioning. Out of fear, the Israelis created more barriers and the Arabs, in turn, grew irritated getting questioned just to buy a loaf of bread. And back and forth it goes. You can see the conundrum. You do that, and then we'll do this. Unending. I started to dread going to work.

My dread turned to fear very quickly, when a fellow Belush member was assassinated. He was from another station, and none of us knew him, but reading the police report was chilling for all of us. He had been taken while on night patrol and tortured for several hours. Then they dragged him by his neck, until just his spine held his body together. No forensic investigators were needed for that crime—the whole thing was taped and sent to police headquarters.

I briefly considered adding a vial of lethal injection to my ammo belt. Police personnel had access to this shot only while on special assignments, with the understanding it could be used upon capture. Perhaps an instant death would be better than torture. I decided my Beretta would work just fine. One shot to the temple should do it. I added another lock to my door at home and another layer to my outer shell.

Just a few weeks later, Rami and I partnered on an evening shift. I leaned my head against the window and watched a group of cyclists ride by. I longed to be one of them. Jac had sent me a letter telling me all about his training and his plan to try professional racing. *Maybe I could do that? Could I actually race my bike and get paid?*

"I'm not sure about this job anymore," I offered.

"What do you mean?" he turned his head toward me, sensing the seriousness.

I was about to tell him. Tell him about my sleepless nights and disgust at human beings. Tell him that I'm afraid now, where I hadn't been before, and tell him that I wanted out.

"I," I stammered, and then stopped. I saw one of our cars parked along the road next to an orange grove, and we slowly pulled up next to it. "Forget it," I said, rolling down my window to check in. Schmoleck and David, the new guy, were sound asleep.

I threw an apple core at their window, "Wake up, you morons! You can't nap out here!"

Not only was it against regulations, but also it's risky. I could barely sleep in my own deadbolted house, let alone on the side of a road in a crappy neighborhood, and here these guys were sleeping like babies. Rami got out and leaned in the window. "Seriously, everything going on right now, and you guys are sleeping? Move along." Schmoleck winked at me and waved us away.

A couple hours later, the sun was just rising as we headed back to the base. I checked my watch. I could speed home, ride for two hours, and still have time to sleep for five. *Perfect.* Then the radio blared.

"Matzav harom! Ahad shalanu." *Assassination. One of ours.*

My spine stiffened and I looked at Rami. His eyes blinked in half-second intervals as he pulled the car onto the shoulder. The radio crackled an address. Rami spun the car around, gunned the engine, and ran every red light across town. But there was really no need to hurry. They were already dead. And we already knew who it was.

Rami skidded to a stop, the red crime scene tape already holding back the morning crowd. I half-jogged over to Schmoleck and David's car. The front windshield was shattered and, at first, I thought the bodies had already been moved. But as I came closer, I could see pieces of flesh and bone on the side windows, seats, and out the back of the car. My heart sank. They had been completely blown away, hundreds of rounds shredding their entire upper bodies. I quickly ducked under the tape and walked over to Rami, Eli, and Roni, our resident comedian officer. But there were no jokes to soften the blow. There was nothing to say. I put my hands in my pockets and took a deep breath.

Anger swept through me. *Who in the hell does this to another human being?* And complete despair, thinking of Schmoleck only one year from retiring. *This will never be over. There is no end. You can only try and contain it.* And fear. *That, of course, could have been me.*

I thought back to my first days in the military, full of patriotism, with no thoughts about actually dying for the cause. Death wasn't scary, although that's probably because I had no experience with it, and in my hotheaded teenage brain, death seemed as unlikely as my going to Mars. I had to step back and really look at my situation. *Why did I intentionally seek such a dangerous profession? Why did I fight so hard for a job that I completely loathe? Why, now, am I afraid to die?*

I took a few days off, and rode my bike harder than I ever had. The thoughts flew through my head as I pedaled against the scorching wind. *Did I really think this would be like a James Bond movie? The car will not fly away if someone shoots at me, I will simply be shot. But am I really going to try and get transferred out? No one does that! Will people think I'm weak? Oh, Schmoleck.*

At night, my ritual of double locking doors and making sure my gun was on the nightstand escalated significantly.

I slept on the living room floor, back against the wall with my Beretta in my hand, loaded and safety off. My spare gun lay similarly on the ground next to my mattress, butt end facing me for a quick grab. My knife stayed strapped to my calf and, honestly, I barely slept.

"I'm not going to fucking debriefing, Rami!" Everyone was trying to get me to go. First day back on the job, and they were all hounding me. I thought it would be useless. How could someone who spends his days behind the safety of a desk possibly have anything to tell me? Rami was still gently trying to convince me, when Bosley called us to his office.

We sat across from him, his small desk scattered with papers and sticky notes. He threw a black and white photograph on top of the mess. It was us. Rami, Eli, Roni, and me, my hands in my pockets, shoulders slightly elevated taking a deep breath. *Crime scene. Someone took our picture?* The photo had just arrived in the mail, with the caption, "You are next."

Strangely, I felt nothing. My nighttime thoughts had already imagined every possible scenario. Capture. Torture. Midnight assassin. They'd all played out during my endless, sleepless nights. Bosley didn't waste time.

"Well, that's it then. You'll all be transferred immediately. Go home for a week and we'll let you know."

I drove straight home and called Yitzik.

All police and security departments constantly train and upgrade skills. Several times a month, a supervisor would come to our post, or we'd go to their base, to work on shooting, self-defense, terrorism scenarios, working with dangerous gases, and more. Yitzik was everyone's favorite trainer, serious and incredibly skilled, but with a warm edge to his eyes that showed his genuine care for us. He had approached me after our first session together, only a few weeks after I'd joined the police force. He'd had our squad run the obstacle course, and I could still kill it.

A total fitness buff, he immediately liked me and signed me up for the Police Games. I won every event I entered, and almost lapped the field in the 1,000-meter run. I was shocked at the poor fitness of the police force, and Yitzik and I would often discuss the situation. He and I both knew unfit cops were more depressed, more stressed, and less proficient at their jobs, and he had started discussing systematic changes with our regional commander, General Borovsky.

I continued my work with the Belush, but started wondering if I'd be happier in a career in fitness. And after seeing my photo on Bosley's desk, I really wanted out.

"Yitzik? It's Leah."

"Yah—Leah. How are you?" His quiet tone revealed that he knew. Everyone knew.

"I've been better. I'm not sure what to do now."

"I do. You'll come work with me. Just give me a week."

Yitzik convinced Borovsky to create a new position for me. I left the Belush and moved forty miles north to the Police Headquarters in Haifa.

I winced. From the memory or the pain, I couldn't tell. "This is not going to work," I mumbled, a sling tucked under my chin.

The crew had devised a suspension system for my head—a sling attached to a PVC pipe that ran down my back. They were trying to figure out how to attach it to my bike or my pants. Neither one seemed plausible, but I stood patiently as they tinkered with it. My pace had fallen so much that we all knew I couldn't break the record, and my closest female competitor was almost a full day behind. We were in no-man's land. After ten minutes though, I couldn't hold my head up any longer.

"Just take it off." My frustration spilled over onto the crew.

I so badly wanted to race—my legs felt great, but the neck pain took away every ounce of strength I had. The constant ache was maddening and sapped my hunger. Plus, I couldn't see the road very well, and had to brake on every descent. The disappointment welled up in me. I felt the rest of the race would be a waste of time, but quitting just wasn't in me.

I clipped my shoe back into the pedal and Ed held my bike steady as I clipped in the other and pushed toward the bridge. *Just pedal.* The Mississippi River flowed under me like a giant brown mudslide. I was over halfway. I was crossing over.

Borovsky, Yitzik, and I at Police Headquarters in Haifa created new standards of fitness for the entire force. I personally trained high-officials and endless groups of police personnel. I lived in a villa less than a block from the beach, making decent money. I was assured of a comfortable retirement at forty-five years old—only sixteen years away.

Although most of my job revolved around fitness, I still got called out for special assignments, raiding houses, and other security "missions." The ugliness of human beings was overwhelming and for the first time in my life I started to feel lonely. Spikee, my dog, was my only companion and I think even she could feel my despair. There was no one to talk to—to understand the work I did. Most evenings, we would walk or run on the beach and I would try to forget everything I'd seen and felt that day. I had to admit, the work had worn me down.

One afternoon, Spikee and I started walking at 2:00 p.m. and the memories of my years in Israel flooded over me. Basic Training, Course Oleem Hadasheem, the police, the Belush—I handled and excelled at each one individually. But now, it seemed the trauma was accumulating. I felt like a prisoner, with very few choices, and a future of more ugliness and danger. Spikee and I walked all the way past Atlit and climbed up on some rocks. The heat of the day started to fade and we sat down to rest.

I looked out over the blue Mediterranean Sea and wondered why I felt so restless. *I have a good job. My home is huge and beautiful—marble floors and amazing views of the beach. But I'm miserable.* My heart felt heavy and empty. I started daydreaming about what it would be like to leave Israel. *Would that mean that I'd failed? That I was a quitter? Could I really go back to Canada and start again? Could I be an athlete again?*

It was after 9:00 p.m. when I tore myself away from fantasyland, and started to walk home. Spikee and I had walked that beach a hundred times, but this time felt different. It seemed as though I had started to walk away—away from a life of violence and insanity. Away from a dictated and lonely life, and had started my journey toward freedom. It was so dark along the water; I had to follow the white spots on Spikee just to keep a straight line. For once, the darkness didn't stir up the fear it normally did. I felt lighter and dared to be the tiniest bit optimistic.

Maybe I could be normal. Maybe I could be like everyone else—a person unaffected by the brutality of humans—just maybe. I slid into bed and tried to close my eyes. It was time to take back my life—to start a new chapter that didn't involve terrorists and rapists. I knew for sure that my time in Israel was coming to an end. I needed to get out—and immediately started dreaming of my next chapter.

Illinois

"Be very, very careful what you put into that head,
because you will never, ever get it out."
Cardinal Thomas Wolsey

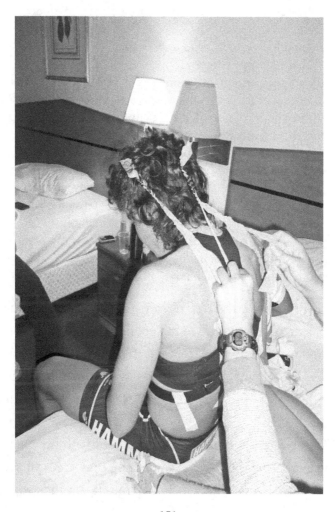

"I got it!" Lori yelled.

I could hear her from where I was inside a porta-potty we'd found on a roadwork site.

"What have ya got?" I asked, propping my head on my chin.

"We can use tensor bandages braided into your hair!"

I had no idea what she was talking about and, after about five other failed ideas, I didn't get my hopes up. I came out, and steadied myself with my bike.

"Just make it four more hours to the hotel. We'll do it there."

I nodded, pretending to understand.

That night, as I slept propped up on every pillow in the room, Lori cut strips of stretchy athletic wrap, and braided it into three sections of my hair. After my pathetic three hours of sleep, Janessa pulled the strips tight and tied them to my heart rate monitor strapped around my ribs. I had to admit—it worked. The pain didn't magically disappear of course, but my head felt lighter and easier to turn. For the first time in days, I actually rode really hard.

Near the end of the day, however, the tension on my skull started to give me a headache. It gradually got worse, and the pain seemed to float between my brain and my neck. *At least it's spread out a bit.* Plus, I could see more of the road, which made all of us feel safer.

I didn't hesitate to tell Yitzik my new plan and although he was disappointed to see me go, he immediately started helping me find my replacement. Borovsky and a few others tried to get me to reconsider, but it was futile. I knew I needed to go. The next challenge was relentlessly calling to me.

I'm consistently shocked and dismayed with how many people describe their life as something they are "trapped" in, or "just living with." It baffles me. It reminds me of those people who always buy the same breed of dog throughout their entire lives. You know who I'm talking about. "Our family has always had German Shepherds." And that's it. It doesn't matter that the family now lives in a concrete jungle, with schedules that would confuse NASA, and absolutely no time for a large, energetic dog. A pet expert might recommend that the family get a fish, or a drought-tolerant plant instead. But no. Their family always has had a German Shepherd.

Perhaps it's habit. Or nostalgia. Or perhaps once we believe something very strongly, we simply can't "un" believe it. Change is scary, I know. I've met so many people living with spouses they don't love (hence my longtime belief that true love doesn't really exist) or in jobs they despise. At least *knowing* the negatives in one's life saves them from the dreaded unknown. And that's what really keeps us trapped, isn't it? The fear of something worse! "Maybe a German Shepherd would dig holes in the yard from lack of exercise, but what if a fish is just impossible to live with? I can't take that chance."

For some, I believe a fear of change stems from an aversion to admitting mistakes. "If I leave my spouse, then that means I screwed up by marrying him or her in the first place." "If the drought-tolerant plant turns out to be the best companion our family has ever had, then that means I was totally wrong about Fido!"

But that's just not true. Change is good—even if you screw up. It means that you're still willing to learn, to grow and, yes, make mistakes.

From the moment I left the Middle East, I felt lighter. There were no bombs in Vancouver. No terror. No gun under my pillow, knife strapped to my leg, and semi-automatic next to the bed. I thought I could sleep in peace here, start over. But I still didn't sleep. I felt lost and suddenly unimportant. Plus, all the years of emotional disengagement had left me tense and rigid. I was always irritated, either snapping at people or completely ignoring them. *I made a huge mistake coming back.*

A cop pulled me over for speeding during my first week of readjustment, and I was pissed. My mind flashed back to a time I was pulled over in Israel. I was still a Belush, and a traffic cop had waved me to the side. I'd been speeding down the shoulder, as I often did, passing the rush hour gridlock so I could get home to my running shoes. As he approached, I shoved my police hat onto the dashboard and gave him a dirty look. *Moron.* He averted his eyes and quickly walked away. I was untouchable. The knock on the window jolted me back to my Canadian reality, and I handed over my license like a common citizen.

That night, my mother sat across from me at their kitchen table, holding a cup of tea. She had offered me one, but I'd shaken my head. She looked hard at me, searching my eyes for something she recognized.

"Where has my daughter gone?" she nearly whispered.

I just tapped the back of her hand, hoping it would make her feel a little better. But I said nothing. I had no answer. I wanted to bust out of my hard shell, but I felt trapped; cold and hollow.

My mother, quietly hopeful that somehow her daughter would reappear contrasted comically with my disappointed father. My military and police ambitions confused him. I could've studied business or law and started making real money without the danger and the sacrifice required in the Middle East. But after rising through the ranks, I'd landed at the prestigious Police Headquarters rubbing elbows with Generals.

He couldn't understand why, after finally getting a "good" job, I quit after only eighteen months. I could see his point. I wasn't completely sure myself. Cavity searches, merry-go-round arrests of drug dealers, and the constant fear of death definitely played their part. But it was even more than that. I felt like I was being swallowed, bit by bit, the darkness threatening to completely overtake me. I'd had to come back.

My father owned a few commercial properties, including a building housing a deli and a car wash. He graciously offered me the job of overseeing his deli. Literally. I managed the place, and he converted the overhead loft into a bachelor apartment that always smelled like roast beef and car wash soap. I couldn't tell my father my real plan; he'd drop dead if I told him I was going to be a cyclist.

At first, I dove into the work, getting a liquor license to increase profits, running specials with the car wash next door, and trying to learn the delicate dance of managing people I couldn't just yell at and demand a hundred push-ups. I'd get up at four-thirty in the morning and workout until seven. I'd spend most of my day behind the counter or in the office, and then try to sneak in an afternoon ride. My father knew I needed a lot of help—I didn't know anything about filing payroll or submitting corporate taxes. He generously offered advice and frequently dropped in to check on things. I wasn't used to taking orders from anyone, however, and I saw his diligence as a misplaced power trip.

We increasingly butted heads, and I found myself avoiding him. He'd call to say he was dropping by, and I'd conveniently have to run out for supplies. He grew weary, explaining time sheets and employee-incentive strategies. And I, stuck in my hard shell, started to boil inside. I couldn't believe I'd traded my high-status job for this. *I am a deli manager. Shit.*

One afternoon, fully engaged in a long moment of self-pity, I heard my father's footsteps pounding up the stairs. *Great.* I slumped in my office chair and glared at the offending room. Four walls surrounded me—my worst nightmare. *I left Israel for this? Maybe he's right—I left too hastily. I just didn't think it through.*

The door swung open and the list of weekly mistakes began. Normally, I would've sat silently, avoided eye contact, and waited for him to finish. But not today. I had reached my limit. I slowly stood to face him and, through clenched teeth, starting verbally pushing him back. My mother had come too, but she stood wide-eyed and silent as her daughter and husband's discussion quickly turned into a yelling match.

"You never should have left Israel! I told you dis job took

a lot of work! You aren't taking it as serious—just letting the workers walk all over you!"

"Are you crazy? I LIVE here! I'm here twelve hours a day! What else can I do?"

"You can try harder! Did you think dis would be easy?"

"No, I didn't think it would be easy—but give me a break! I'm doing my best!"

"This—is your best?"

And that was it. I charged toward him and he quickly backed up against the wall. My mother grabbed his sleeve, trying to pull him toward the door, but it was too late. I threw my fist right past his unbelieving eyes. My knuckles smashed through the drywall and started to bleed. I coiled my arm up again. *To do what? Actually hit him?*

My mother grabbed me and whispered, "You go now," looking at me as if I were a stranger. I took the stairs down two at a time and ran to my car. My mother didn't even recognize what I had become—a hollow human with only anger inside. I drove back to the one person who might understand all this—who knew what I'd been through and how it had changed me. The one person I still considered a friend—Jac.

We had reconnected the previous month, and while neither of us wanted to rekindle our romantic relationship, we fell back into a comfortable friendship. After the argument with my father, he let me move in with him, and he suggested we go shopping. At the time, La Bicicletta was the biggest bike store in the city, the place where most serious cyclists bought their gear. Jac took me there, eager to get me on a decent bike so he'd have a riding partner. He told me of his plan to become a professional, and urged me to train with him and see what could happen. The rows and rows of cycling gear in the store were overwhelming.

Jac picked out a black Cramerotti for me. It was within my price range of $500, and had a dinner plate-sized cassette. The cassette is the big metal circle between your pedals—it has teeth on it to pull the chain around—the larger the size, the easier the gears. So, when I climbed a steep hill, I would be able to gear down enough to still move forward. Jac was powerful and light and, therefore, a great climber. I think he was nervous I would get left behind if he didn't set me up with easy gears.

The rest of the bike was not brag-worthy. The heavy steel frame sat on too-fat tires with below-average hardware and components. I didn't know any of this was important at the time, of course. As far as I knew, a bike was a bike. I called a coach, a local rider named Barb Morris, and explained my background in duathlon, my plan to transition into cycling, and asked if she could help me get there.

Barb agreed, but first insisted on a home visit to check out my equipment. I grudgingly invited her to my parents' house in Vancouver. I never liked people to know where I lived, but Barb insisted that my success depended on having the proper gear. In Israel, any new advance in sports equipment had seemed to take ten years to finally appear. I knew my stuff wasn't the best, and I was completely clueless when it came to components, frames, and shoes. As Barb's trained eye glared at my crates full of cycling gear, it was quickly evident how clueless I really was.

My black Cramerotti bike sat idly on my trainer. I still

hadn't grown accustomed to the cold weather and rain, so I often rode indoors. My hair-dryer helmet (as I came to learn it was called) hung over one of the handlebars. Barb's face fell into a polite shock. "How much does that bike weigh?" she asked.

I have absolutely no idea. "It's pretty light," I replied. In truth, the sucker weighed twenty-five pounds—a big, fat, sturdy bike. It would be great for commuters or Pee Wee Herman, but not for a racer. I actually crashed that Cramerotti a couple months later. I slid sideways on black ice and ended up with torn gloves and thirteen stitches in my head. But that bike didn't even lose a chip of paint. Yep, really sturdy. My hair-dryer helmet, thankfully, managed to crack and had to be replaced. It's called a hair-dryer helmet because it looks like one of those old-fashioned hair dryers your grandmother used to sit under. Yes, it's that big.

"Where is your floor pump?"

"What's a floor pump?"

In Israel, I used a small hand pump. I'd push air in and then squeeze the tire with my thumb. When it felt hard, I'd stop. Simple.

She smiled. "You need it to properly inflate your tires. They look low."

She crossed the room and picked up my bike. "Is this the bike you plan to race with?"

"Yes."

"Oh, my. Well, you may want to consider replacing it at some point. Your bike is not really a racing bike." I wasn't sure exactly what that meant, but it didn't sound good.

Several other riders had recommended Barb, and I have to give her credit, she was a great starter coach for me. We'd meet for rides several times a week and she was always in teaching mode; explaining the endless intricacies and complexities of racing a bike.

"Cycling is a chess game. You can't just ride faster than everyone else and expect to win—you have to be smarter than everyone else too. In a race, your greatest asset is the *peloton*," she explained. This French term, referring to a small platoon of cyclists in a group, is used to describe the way cyclists stay together to cut through the wind like a flock of geese. The pack will always be faster than an individual rider. Each rider is expected to take a turn at the front, fighting the wind and leading the pack, until they start to tire and pull aside. Another rider moves to the front and "pulls" for the group, and on it goes.

Barb told me about the importance of teamwork, and that it's nearly impossible to win a multi-day stage race alone. She explained the backroom deals teams even made with each other, offering up riders to help another team win a stage if they reciprocated the next day. The first few months of information overwhelmed me, and I was grateful to have a coach.

Not long after I crashed my Cramerotti, not even long enough for me to buy a better helmet, Barb invited me to a Wednesday group ride with some local pro riders. Barb and I had trained together for months, and the cycling etiquette rules were starting to sink in. I pulled into the meeting spot, a parking lot in Burnaby, and immediately wondered if I was ready for this.

Men and women in perfectly matching cycling outfits stood in small groups, talking and laughing, holding their gleaming, skinny bikes with one hand. I heaved out my fat Cramerotti and cracked hairdryer helmet and scanned the crowd for Barb. Thankfully, she saw me first and was already walking toward me. We wheeled our bikes toward the twenty-something riders while she gave me last-minute instructions.

"Don't feel intimidated, Leah. The pace is going to be really fast, but I want you to try to do your part. Stay in the peloton and, if you can, take your turn pulling at the front." She introduced me to a few people, including Alyson Syder, a mountain biker who had an Olympic medal and a World Championship under her belt. Barb said her name as if I should know her, but I'd spent the last twelve years in the desert; I barely knew who Oprah was.

I rode with them, furiously pushing my legs and heaving my lungs just to maintain their pace. I stayed tucked into the group most of the ride, trying to draft and not get dropped. People spoke to each other, but only briefly. No one, however, uttered a word to me. Eventually, I thought I should take my turn at the front, and slowly, painfully made my way close to the leaders until I came shoulder to shoulder with one of the front female riders. She looked over at me, staring for just a little too long. I glanced over. *Yeah?*

"You don't belong up here," she said, her eyes back on the

road. She flicked her left hand, showing me the way to the back, as if her words weren't clear enough. *Wow, friendly crowd.* I hung on for two hours, and then thankfully I had to split off and go to work. I couldn't believe the pace they held on a training ride, and I wearily pedaled back to my car. The next day, I asked Barb if she had seen my encounter with the blonde.

"Oh, yeah—that was Leslie Tomlinson." *Still. No idea.*

"Why did she tell me to move?" I asked, indignant at the treatment and wondering just who these people thought they were.

"Welcome to cycling," she offered, smiling. "There's definitely a pecking order. A hierarchy. These riders are some of the best in the world. You have to put in the work and time to climb your way to the top. They've already done their time, and often they like to remind a newcomer where their place is."

Really? People win a stupid bike race and suddenly think they are superior human beings? It's just cycling. They aren't pedaling their insanely overpriced bikes in an effort to save humanity or anything!

That's what I thought back then. But by the time I worked my way up to the front of the peloton and won stupid bike races, I started to feel myself inflate. I learned quickly that new riders tend to make mistakes, leave gaps, and cause crashes. Occasionally, I'd even catch a glimpse of my own hand waving a rookie to the back.

"It's a five-year commitment. Sure you're up for it?" Barb snapped me out of my mental rant.

"Yeah. I'm up for it."

Cyclists are odd, overly self-important people for the most part. I swear that's half the reason I stuck with the crazy sport those first few years. I felt like I had to show them up, to try to pop some inflated heads. But I also got hooked, obsessed even, because the sport turned out to be so damn hard.

The next few years, I concentrated all my effort on the bike, but I still needed an income. My father and I weren't speaking; I couldn't work full time and still train like I wanted, and I quickly discovered just how expensive good bike equipment was. I had enough money saved up to get me through a year, but after that, I'd need a high income, low-commitment job. I called David.

I'd met David (I'm sure that's not his real name) during my last year in Israel, and we'd had several conversations that started with him recruiting me to work undercover among Neo-Nazis in North America, and ending with me saying no. My job would be to infiltrate gangs and report information back to Dave. I had no interest. He thought I was perfect—blonde, athletic, pale; I looked more like the Master Race than a typical Israeli Jew. But just thinking about tattoos, alcohol, and partying all night made my head spin and were as foreign to me as ice ballet.

"Even if I wanted to work for you, Dave, I just couldn't pull that off, acting like that."

"We would teach you everything you need to know."

I've never even had a sip of beer. "Nobody's that good," I'd joke, while remembering the time I'd posed as a prostitute with the Belush. We'd all laughed about that one for months. I wasn't an actor. Plus I had no intention of reinserting myself into a violent and dangerous job.

"Well, you call me if you ever need work in North America," he'd said. "Perhaps we could find something else for you."

So I called him and asked what else there was.

"Secure transport."

"What's that," I asked.

"I tell you when and where to pick something up, and when and where to drop it off. That's it."

He didn't elaborate and I didn't ask questions. *We are Israelis—we don't ask questions. People? Money? Weapons?* I decided it didn't matter—at least I knew the type of operations he ran, and that I would be helping fight skinheads anyway. He assured me I could work when I wanted, nothing illegal or overly dangerous, but that most of the jobs would be in the United States.

"No problem. I'll tell you when I can start." I explained my cycling ambitions and assumed eventually I'd be racing in the U.S., and he replied, "Perfect."

The first year, I was a Category 4 rider—the bottom of the 1, 2, 3, and 4 divisions, riding in races with Barb and a few others from Seymour Cycles, a bike shop in North Vancouver. My very first race, the Harris-Roubaix in Langley, was set up like a European road race, with sharp corners and lots of gravel in an attempt to mimic cobblestone streets. It was a fairly small women's field, so all levels rode together. Barb told me that if I could stay with the lead peloton, and drop the rest of the Category 4 riders, then I would "lead her out" close to the finish, so she could win the Category 1 division.

"Leading out" requires a teammate to sprint all-out, while another "sits in," tucked behind the leader's wheel. The front rider burns out her legs and lungs for 200 meters or so, and then the rear rider slingshots out of the wind pocket and flies to the finish. It requires sacrifice. In my case, it didn't matter if Barb beat me—we were in different categories—and honestly, I couldn't have beat her anyway. But at higher levels, teammates "slingshot" their top rider to the finish all while sacrificing their own chance of winning.

It all went according to plan, and we both won our divisions. The organizer came up to me after the race.

"So you're our Category 4 winner, huh? Well, I guess we'd better get you something!" He dug around in a cardboard box on the ground and emerged with a white plastic water bottle.

"Congrats!" he smiled. It seems ridiculous now, but I was so happy with that water bottle. I didn't even use it for years. I watched Barb get the Category 1 prize, and I knew I had to work harder.

I wanted to be the leader. But it was just a thought. A distant dream. I had a lot to learn first.

Jac started taking me to the Saturday Knight Street ride, a blistering fast group-ride of pros (and wannabes) through the Vancouver suburbs. The first week, I got dropped within six miles. I couldn't keep up. The next week I tried to draft more, and got dropped after ten. Each week I'd learn a little more strategy or technique from Barb and each Saturday, full of hope and energy, I'd get "popped" from the Saturday group ride. It was maddening.

Jac started ribbing me about not being able to keep up. It actually started to irritate me, so one day I said, "Just wait. Someday, I will beat you." He said something about dying a slow and painful death before that would ever happen, and we didn't discuss it again. Most people would probably just join a different group ride, or just train alone; but not me. I showed up on Saturdays—and got dropped every time—for an entire year.

And then one Saturday, I made it. I survived the Saturday group ride and I was as happy as I had been with my Harris-Roubaix water bottle. I put my forehead on my hands, leaning over my bike, and savored the small victory. Before I even had time to catch my breath, an ex-pro, Roger Sumner, wheeled his bike up next to me.

"I knew you'd make it eventually, Leah. Why don't you come out and train with the British Columbia Provincial Team?" he offered, in his proper English accent. He helped scout and coach up-and-coming riders. I agreed, and started a training camp in Victoria the following spring. I improved quickly, and a few of the coaches mentioned sending me to Europe with the Canadian Development Team. I didn't really know what that would entail, but I wanted to keep learning and improving. If that meant going to France, I was game.

At the end of the camp, Victoria hosted the Canadian Cycling Association Awards banquet, and the riders and coaches buzzed about who would be there, and who to talk to.

"Pierre will be here—it'll be a great time to introduce yourself," Roger commented. He coached my pro team, Soloton, and knew most of the coaches and directors associated with the national program.

"Who's that?" I lied. I'd heard the name several times, as Canadian riders complained about his selection process. He was a Frenchman, with no racing background—he was really a manager and logistics guy. But his consistent favoritism toward Quebec and Ontario riders hadn't made him any friends on the West Coast.

"He's the President of the Association. He'll play a big role in the advancement of your career. In other words— you want him to like you. You need to go to this event."

Great. Politics? Plus a large crowd, small talk with strangers, and a table full of food I won't eat? Sounds like a nightmare. I still went to the banquet.

I picked at my plate of cantaloupe and grapes while Sandy Esposeth, a more experienced development rider, scanned the crowd. We'd trained together much of the summer and were content to just sit in the corner and talk about European racing.

"It's nothing like here," she said, shaking her head. "Nothing."

"What do you mean?"

"You'll see," she said, already convinced that I would be picked for the National Development Team.

I looked to the middle of the room, and saw a tall, graying

man surrounded by young women. *That's gotta be Pierre.* He carried his 6' 3" frame with an almost ludicrous air of self-importance, keeping his long nose slightly elevated so he always appeared to be looking down. Potential national riders buzzed around him, like drones fanning the queen. The hairs on the back of my neck stood up.

"You should go introduce yourself," Sandy tried to give me sage advice.

"What?" I never felt comfortable meeting new people, and his pompous demeanor made me squirm. I understood his role in my future as a cyclist, and although racing my bike had become my new obsession, I couldn't connect socializing with sport.

"No, thanks." *If he wants to meet me, he knows where to find me.*

"Let's go, Leah," Roger popped me out of my daydream. He pulled my chair out and led me over to Pierre.

"This is necessary. Smile," he whispered. I did, and the quick introduction took less than thirty seconds. The next spring, I started planning my move to France. *He must have liked my fake smile.*

This road is worse than any cobblestone crap in Europe! My bike rattled over the chewed-up pavement, shooting waves of pain through my neck and back. Work crews lined both sides of the road, and traffic funneled into one lane. The cars, inches from my handlebars, rolled along so slowly I had to pass them. But I was forced into the rough shoulder. I'd been riding in it for over an hour.

My follow vehicle had fallen way behind me. *Oh, my God, how many more days of this?* I stood up on my pedals. I had developed a serious saddle sore, and the numbing cream I'd been abusing was wearing off. A saddle sore emerges from too much pressure and friction in one area—just like a bedsore. I'm sure I don't have to tell you where mine was.

I couldn't see the end of the construction, my head and neck throbbed from the added movement, and I swore out loud every time I sat. Suddenly, I just snapped.

I pulled over further to the right, alongside the edge of the road. I unclipped, stepped off, and heaved my bike into the bushes. It landed softly, suspended on its side with branches sticking through the frame and wheels. I sat down on the crappy road, cursing their existence. *Bikes and roads. Who comes up with this shit? Did I just swear? When did I start doing that?*

I sat in my pathetic state of self-pity, contemplating a few other ridiculous items. *Why can we put a man on the moon, but can't make roads that last more than a season? Just finish this race. Last one. My Shimano shoes are so comfy. No one will ever cheer for me again. I have to pee.* Ten minutes seemed to be enough. I wrenched my bike back out of the shrubbery, wheeled it onto the gravel, and clipped back in. *What other choice do I have?*

INDIANA

*"Don't say you don't have enough time. You have exactly
the same number of hours per day that were given to Helen
Keller, Pasteur, Michelangelo, Mother Teresa, Leonardo
da Vinci, Thomas Jefferson, and Albert Einstein."*
H. Jackson Brown, Jr. *Life's Little Instruction Book*

"Car back," Sean came through on the radio.

I slid my bike slightly further to the right, making it
easier for the car coming up behind to pass me. Cyclists
and race follow-cars constantly use this phrase—it's a
safety warning. My crew really had to stay on top of me
now, as occasionally I'd ride closer to the middle of the
road than the shoulder. They also radioed stop signs,
sharp turns, railroad tracks, and "Car Up," meaning a
car was headed toward me. They didn't trust my brain
at all. And for that stuff, they couldn't.

My mind, preoccupied with pain and memories,
wasn't reacting to real-life happenings very quickly.

"Leah—do you want Perpetuem® [a supplement
drink] or an energy bar? You have to eat something!"
Sean again.

Ew. I'd eaten so much of both those things, I couldn't
imagine swallowing one more ounce. *Maybe I could
think of something that would taste good. Think. Think.*

"Leah!" Sean. Again. *Did I not answer him?* "We're
going to pass you a Perpetuem® at the next hand off."

I half nodded and sure enough, half a kilometer up
the road Janessa and Sean stood in the shoulder about
200 meters apart. And just as we'd done a hundred times
prior, I threw my old bottle to Janessa and grabbed a

new one from a running Sean. I pretended to take a drink and then shoved it into a holder. *I'll dump that out later.*

Janessa encouraging me to eat more.

"How long are you going to keep this up," my father asked, referring to my newly started cycling career.

"As long as it takes."

After two years of me and my father not speaking, my mother had finally gotten us in the same room. I felt anxious; after not seeing him in so long, I wasn't sure what to expect. As soon as I'd come through the door he crossed the room and pulled me into a huge hug. We stayed like that for several seconds—definitely a record. He said nothing, nor did I. Family always forgives, and it felt good to talk to him again. It only took a few hours though, before he started talking about a "real" job. I had to smile. *At least I always know where I stand with my father.*

"Really, Dad. I just want to see how far I can take this." I never understood timelines exactly. Goals, I get. Dreams—totally. But why have a time limit? I wanted something and, therefore, was willing to commit to getting it. Period.

I spent the next two springs in Europe racing with the Development Team, which is another way of saying the "B" team. The "A" team, with Clara Hughes and Alyson Syder raced in World Cup races, Commonwealth Games, and the Olympics. The "B" team was sent to race on the French Cup circuit, assimilating to the blistering speed and take-no-prisoners peloton.

I met the other six development riders in Paris, all of them timid and very young. The ages ranged from fourteen to twenty-one, except for me. I was thirty. A team manager, a Frenchman named Christian, met us at the airport upon arrival. He looked us all up and down.

"Well, you are all too fat." He alleged. "Welcome to France."

Canadians are nice. The young riders were stunned and hurt by this type of language. But I'd dealt with straight-talking Israelis for the past ten years; it didn't bother me at all. Besides, he was right. After getting the best components, the lightest bike, and possessing great fitness, the biggest determinant of cycling power output is weight.

"Why do you spend $4,000 on the lightest frame—when you still 'ave to pull an extra ten pounds up the Alps?" Christian would yell, throwing his hands up. After one especially terrible finish, he told the team that there would be no dinner. We drove in silence, the girls desperately looking at one another. I convinced Christian to stop at the grocery store, which he grudgingly did.

"You 'ave five minutes," he steamed.

I knew these girls wouldn't last long. European coaches are brutal taskmasters, and the races are battles—physically and verbally. I saw spitting, hair pulling, swearing, and a few full-face slaps. A rider grabbing another's arm and pushing her back was very common. In one of my first French Cup races, a Spanish cyclist put her hand on me, preparing to push me back. I slapped it away.

"Your hand touches me again, you're going to lose it," I stated, calmly and honestly. She believed me.

Riders earn respect on the race circuit by results, great bike handling skills, and even fear. I had a slight advantage, as rumors spread about me on both sides of the ocean. "I heard she was a Commando soldier!" "No, she worked undercover for Israel, and she's killed seven people!" Stuff like that. I rarely corrected them. The fear gave me a little more room in the peloton.

I slowly adjusted to the speed, and started finishing top ten, and then top five. During my second season, I'd won several single day races and a stage race. Roger called me.

"Good news! I think you're going to race the Tour de France!" he exclaimed. I knew the female version had another name, and wasn't quite as long as the men's race, but was long, hilly, and notoriously difficult.

"What? That's a mistake—I'm not ready for something like that."

"Too bad. If they want you, you go. You can't pass up the

opportunity!" he instructed.

I didn't actually believe the Canadian Cycling Association (CCA) would slot me, a development rider, into the biggest stage race in the world. I put it out of my mind and went back to racing.

In one French Cup race, I crashed and fractured a vertebra in my low back. With 300 meters to go, I was sprinting with the leaders including the favorite, Frenchwoman Marion Clignet. One of her Fanini teammates edged closer to me. I felt strong. *I could win this one.* I tucked closer to the wheel in front of me. *Use the slingshot.* Her teammate, riding beside me, knew exactly what I was doing. With 200 meters to go, she slammed her elbow into my arm, causing my handlebars to wobble. My front tire went sideways, and I launched into the air, did a front flip, and landed on my back. I lost all feeling in my legs; they stopped the race and paramedics raced me to the hospital.

I spent a week lying face up in a tiny hospital near Paris where the numbness slowly turned to pain, and the doctors assured me that there were no other serious injuries, but that the fracture required lying flat for a couple weeks. My team carried on to the next race, leaving me with non-English speaking nurses who chain smoked and brought me a plethora of painkillers, which I mostly hid under the mattress. After six sleepless nights, our French team director Christian came and told me a taxi would pick me up in the morning.

"Pierre doesn't want to keep paying for the hospital. You can rest up at my house." *Awesome.*

I traded the plastic back brace for a cloth sleeve, and

went to his house to recuperate. The young girls were horrified at my condition, and even more so when Christian announced that Pierre wanted me to race in three days.

"But I'm on painkillers. I don't think I'm allowed to race," I protested.

"There's no drug testing at this event. Besides, you have a doctor's note. Just don't crash," he added, nodding toward the equipment room. I pulled out a spare, crappy bike and back-up hairdryer helmet, since mine was completely cracked, and grudgingly swallowed another blue pill. On the way to the starting line, my teammates whispered to me.

"Just don't race, Leah. It's not worth it."

"Just start the race and pull out. Pretend your bike broke down."

It wouldn't be a stretch with this old thing.

"Don't worry—it'll be fine," I said, not wanting to race, but not wanting to seem weak.

At the starting line, Christian yelled at me, "Just go hard, Leah!"

So I did. I took off like a rocket, and five other riders broke with me. We created a small lead peloton, and stayed at the lead. After an hour, we continued to separate from the main group and I, fearing another crash, stayed at the front. Christian pulled up beside me in our team car.

"What in the hell are you doing? You are working too hard! Let them pull too!"

But I couldn't. They didn't seem fast enough for me, so I held my lead and just got out-sprinted at the finish. *2nd place.* The second stage of the race was an afternoon time trial, which I managed to win despite not being able to bend over onto my aero bars. I had to admit Christian was right—painkillers helped.

The few girls remaining were sent back to Canada, except me. Christian was so impressed I had raced injured, that he kept me to train for the next big race.

A few weeks later, I joined Canada's "A" team for the Grande Boucle Féminine Internationale, the "Women's Tour de France." The coaches felt I was ready to be a "domestique"—a worker for the top riders representing Canada. Every team has a hierarchy: one or two GC (General Classification) riders—the best overall riders with the best chance of winning a stage race—and specialty riders who could win a time trial or criterium (sprint) stage, but who, for the rest of the race, are domestiques. And of course, there's a pecking order even among them.

I don't think the Canadian coaches expected much from me, but I wanted to do my job. In multi-day stage races, domestiques pedal farther and harder than the GCs—dropping out of the protection of the peloton to fetch water and food from the follow car and fighting the wind alone to deliver it. If the GC gets a flat tire, a domestique gives up her bike and waits for the follow car to bring her another one. It's a tough, often thankless job.

The morning of the first stage, I rode out next to Alyson Syder swallowing down my nerves. She and Sandy Espeseth were our GC riders and it was my job to get them to the finish line in the highest position possible. The first day of long stage races often starts in an unofficial "neutral" pace. The riders glide out of town, waving at the fans and saving the serious speed for later in the race. But not in the Tour. Within minutes, my heart rate was nearly at threshold. I turned to Alyson.

"Holy shit! I thought this was a neutral start!"

She half smiled. "Oh, Leah. We haven't even started racing."

I panted and heaved for air, while the Lithuanians, Germans, and Italians casually chatted. The pace, incredibly fast, seemed to not faze them at all. Halfway through the first day, I crashed and cracked my helmet and wasn't sure I would be able to catch back up to the peloton. But I did, and finished the stage under time cut (the maximum allowable time to finish). And the next day. And the next. Seventeen stages in fourteen days.

Each day, I actually felt more confident; fitter. By the last few days of the race, I was the only domestique still able to help Alyson and Sandy—the others were barely hanging on at the back of the pack. The race pushed me to my limits, but I'd managed to do my job and help our GCs to a respectable finish. Every Canadian finished the race that year—the only country to do so.

I came back to Canada like a machine. B.C. Cup and smaller U.S. races felt like training rides, my body pedaling in insane European speed while many of my competitors rode a friendly North American pace. I was fast and winning; I assumed I'd start getting assignments to represent Canada in World Cup races or Commonwealth Games. But neither happened. I really wanted to make the World Championship team, and after a third-place time-trial finish at the National Championships, I was sure this would be my year.

At the completion of the nationals, I went back to my trade team while the CCA decided my fate. Almost all national riders are employed by a company-sponsored (trade) team throughout the year, and only meet up with the Canadian team for specific races. World Championship riders were picked based on their performance throughout the entire season, not just at a National Podium, but I felt sure my strong season combined with that time trial would assure me a ticket to Portugal. *But will Pierre pick me?*

I knew I wasn't one of his favorites. He'd come to France occasionally to "check in" with the national riders—which meant driving his convertible to cafes and sipping wine with his girlfriend, while we rode the hilly roads to meet him. We'd sometimes finish our ride, only to wait outside in the rain or blistering heat while they finished their espressos. I never spoke out, but kept my distance from him. I never could summon that fake smile again.

About two weeks after the Nationals, the official phone call came from the Federation.

"Bonjour, Ms. Goldstein. We are 'appy to announce some very good news for you!" the overly happy voice exclaimed.

This must be a sales call. "Oh, yeah?" I replied, preparing to hang up.

"On behalf of the National Cycling Federation, I would like to congratulate you on qualifying to represent Canada at the World Championships!"

Relief. Finally Pierre recognized my potential and

trusted me for this assignment. Or perhaps Pierre couldn't find anyone else to send. I'd heard from Roger that I'd been selected for the Tour only because they couldn't find anyone else. The Tour rules state that a team must start the race with seven riders—and the Federation had had trouble finding a seventh man.

"Pierre didn't even think you'd make it two days!" Roger had told me. He meant it as a compliment. It was rare for such a rookie to survive the Tour, but I was reminded that cycling was political. And perhaps our president didn't really believe in me.

Canada, noticeably short on time trialists, possibly couldn't find anyone else to send to the Worlds either. Or maybe my National finish compelled him to send me. I didn't care. I got to compete at the World Championships and, largely, with no expectations. I figured the Federation's hopes would ride on Anne Samplonius, a more seasoned and accomplished rider.

Anne had just finished tenth in an invite-only World Cup Time Trial—an outstanding finish for a Canadian at that time. She was our team's best hope for a top ten finish in any of the disciplines, for men or women. We were about the same age, but she had about ten years of experience on me. *All the pressure is on her.*

My own internal pressure, however, started building. *How many chances will you get at Worlds? Everything has to be perfect.* One of the CCA coaches, with whom I was unfamiliar, called me about a month before I was to fly out.

"Pierre has requested that you take only one bike to the

Worlds," the French-accented woman stated.

Silence. *Crap, he's not going to use me in the road race.* "So, I can only take my time trial bike?" I asked, hoping she was mistaken. I expected to support Sandy and Anne in that race as well.

"No. You will only need your road bike."

Relief. They must have a mix up. "No, I'm in the time trial," I replied, positive she would recheck her papers and see that she had either said the wrong bike or called the wrong person.

"Yes, I know. Pierre wishes you to bring just your road bike. The time trial course is very hilly, so you won't need your TT bike."

I stood with the phone to my ear in dumbfounded silence. Rarely would someone race a time trial with a road bike—especially at a World Championship. I mumbled something half-polite to the woman and hung up. Later that day, I met Roger for a training ride and I was incredulous.

"Can you believe the nerve of that guy? I don't know why I'm surprised—Pierre totally has it in for me."

Roger, attempting to calm me down, replied, "Maybe Pierre is right. That the course is so hilly, you'll have a better shot on a road bike. You do like to stand when you climb." The design of a TT bike discourages standing to pedal as the frame is so compact that the rider's knees hit the handlebars.

He was right, of course, but that didn't comfort me. "You stand when you climb, too! If it was you, and you were being instructed to do an international race on the wrong bike, would you be so calm?"

He had tried. We rode in silence.

Over the coming weeks, Roger spoke with a few of the national coaches to try and get my "bike orders" changed, but to no avail. And finally with only a few days before I flew out, I made a desperate call to Pierre.

"Pierre, I really want to take my time trial bike," I said, trying to get the right mix of confidence and false respect into my voice. Pierre, in my opinion, appreciated people who could keep his feelings of self-importance inflated. It didn't come naturally to me.

"I've heard, Leah, but believe me—you don't need it. The course is hillier than the road race, if you can believe that! Anne's not bringing her TT bike either."

I felt my spine relax.

"Really? She's not?" Definitely a favorite of Pierre's, Anne taking a single bike to Worlds changed everything. If she was taking only one bike, I certainly had no room to complain.

"Many riders will be on road bikes for this—it really is that hilly."

I thanked Pierre, and immediately started packing for the trip. Making lists and piles of gear calms my nerves and centers my attention. As I pulled out my duffle bags and clothing, I tried to put my over-active imagination to rest. *Don't assume the worst in people, Leah. You really don't know all the facts.* And I didn't. All I had was my gut at that point.

I'm a meticulous packer, triple checking every piece of gear. Six bike shorts, seven jerseys, ten pairs of socks, rain gear, two helmets, leg and arm warmers, and a selection of gel gloves. I disassembled my road bike the day before my flight and wedged it into a hard-case bike box. I filled the extra space around the bike with casual clothing, basic tools, and two pairs of bike shoes. I carefully covered my two spare wheels with foam and stacked them in their wheel box. Race food, like gels and powders traveled in a large see-through bag, along with my instant coffee from Israel, chamomile tea for evenings, and sugar-free hot chocolate. My routine of packing is the beginning of warm-up. *Calming and centering.*

I started to believe Pierre was right, and that other riders might be making the same choice—to use a road bike in the hilly Time Trial World Championship. I stepped off the plane in Lisbon feeling fit, and daring to allow myself a small bit of excitement. The next morning, I rolled my bike out of my room and into the large common room. My stomach dropped. Straight ahead of me was Anne. And she had her TT bike.

As I walked toward her, she couldn't take her eyes off my bike, nor could I take mine off hers.

"What the hell?" I said, a bit too loudly.

"Why do you have your road bike, Leah?" she replied, confused. Her face said it all. This was the World Championships, and it was as if I had shown up with training wheels.

"That bastard told me this was all I could bring!" I managed under my breath. And I started to speculate.

If I placed in the top twenty, Canada would have to "card"

me. Many different sports have a process by which athletes with potential to represent Canada (on the international stage) are helped with a stipend. Sport Canada gives these athletes money, access to national coaches, and reduced rates on massage, etc. *Maybe Pierre doesn't want to card me?* It would've meant a salary of $1,500 a month, which isn't much, but would've allowed me the freedom to continue training full time (and working less for David). Plus, it would be more difficult for Pierre to justify keeping me home for international events. I hated to think that this was actually happening, but I couldn't think of any other explanation.

I think other riders in the National Program had noticed Pierre's lack of confidence in me too, but this was a shocking betrayal. In my mind, he had sent me like a lamb to the slaughter, a manipulation to guarantee my failure on the international stage. I couldn't interpret it any other way. My fists closed in anger as I attempted to understand what I had done to deserve this duplicity. Even Anne's eyes seemed to show a flash of pity. In that moment, standing across from my teammate's tripped-out TT bike, I started to consider leaving the Canadian Cycling Program. But first, I had a race.

I shoved my bike back in my room and went to find our team coach, Juri.

I had to explain the situation to him twice, partly because I was speaking so fast, and partly because he didn't believe what he was hearing. "What in the hell is he thinking?" After a long pause, Juri advised me to just make my road bike as aero as possible. "You will have to add aero bars, disc wheels, and adjust your seat." There were no other options. I just had to make the best of the situation.

Switching a road bike into a time trial bike is like trying to make your Jeep run like a Ferrari. Road bikes are light (about sixteen pounds back then, fourteen now), versatile, and are great for climbing, descending, and riding in a crowd. They are easier to maneuver, safer in the wind, and are more comfortable on a long ride. Time trial bikes are heavier (about twenty pounds back then, sixteen now), although still light compared your old 12-speed in the garage. The extreme aerodynamic design of the TT bike allows a greater average speed on a relatively flat, fast course. The frame, wheels, and seat position are all wind tunnel tested to provide the least wind resistance possible. Even the gear shifters are positioned out on the end of the aero bars, so the rider needn't spend a second out of their tucked position. Even subtle changes in the slope of the road require quick gear changes to maximize power output, and I would be forced to reach out of my position every time I shifted.

Our team mechanic spent hours switching equipment, and tweaking my Bianchi road bike to make it as fast as possible. My current professional team director Peter hooked me up with the best frame he could find. "After all, you're going to the Worlds!" he'd said.

I was grateful to have him in my corner. But I still fumed about the frame.

"Maybe he actually thinks you'll do better on a road bike,

since climbing's not really your thing," Sandy offered, trying to lighten my sour mood. She said it in the same way a cyclist would comment on your tires, or components such as your chain ring, derailleur, or brakes.

Pro cyclists have no choice in their equipment—sponsors give it and we use it. My climbing ability was another of those things. Predetermined. A given. *Climbing's not really your thing.* Sandy meant to soften my mood, but I stored that comment in my fuel tanks. I could use that. *She's right.*

Juri expected two things from me—somehow crank out a top thirty finish in the time trial event and support Sandy as best I could on the road race. Our team trained separately, each member following his or her personal coach's program. I went for a few fast rides, readjusting to the narrow European roads.

Anne and I spent extra time studying the TT course. We discussed the course, and shared ideas on strategy, as if we were at a business meeting discussing profit margins and stock options. Anne, serious and focused, was there to do a job, not make friends and chat at cafes. We, therefore, made good teammates. Quiet. Serious. Focused. Amen.

The course was hilly, Pierre had been right about that. In the days leading up to the race, I rode every inch of that road about a dozen times. The pitch of the pavement, the cracks in the centerline, and optimal routes into the corners were all studied and noted. All week, riders from all over the world, did the same. And not a damn one of them was on a road bike. Go figure.

On race day, I rode my guts out and managed a fifteenth

place finish—just nipping out Anne who finished in six-teenth. It was one of my proudest moments.

I could still feel the elation of that day. *I competed with the best in the world.* I sat on a curb and watched Rob pump gas, my spare bikes racked on the roof and the van covered with signs and sponsors. *Still looks clean.* I hate dirty cars. Lori sat down beside me and handed me a Tylenol and an orange Gatorade. She looked tired. They all did.

"How are you?" I asked.

"How am I? Let's just worry about you. Only a few more states to go."

She looked defeated. *Was I letting them all down?* Truth was we were in no-man's land. Even if I pedaled backward, I would win, and even if I strapped on a jetpack I wouldn't break the record. Their motivation to make me ride faster was waning, and I could feel the tension between them. Two weeks is a long time to ask a group of strangers to work in close quarters with little sleep and stressful conditions.

Just then, an old guy with a white beard, tattered tank top, and John Deere cap shuffled up to us.

"Are them things bikes?" he asked, pointing to the Trek frames on the roof.

I love Americans. They're so entertainingly nosey.

"Yep," Lori answered.

"Them things expensive? Looks like ya'll got a thousand dollars' worth of stuff settin' up there." *Try about $15,000.*

"Yeah, they are. You'd think they'd go faster," I joked.

"Ya'll in some kind of race or somethin'?"

"Yeah, something like that," Lori said, pointing at me. "She's got a little farther to go."

"Okay then, little lady, git yourself back on that bike and go, go, go!"

We laughed as he walked away, and I wobbled back

to my feet.

"Good thing you didn't tell him how far we're going,"
I said, "he might have had a heart attack."

I smiled and clipped back in. I pushed off, back onto
the road and back into my memories.

Shortly after Sport Canada sent me my treasured "card," I
contacted the Israeli Team Director. I knew they were eager
to build their new national program, and I wanted to keep
my options open if Canada continued to overlook me.

I had another good season with my trade team the following year, and finished second in the 2002 National Time
Trial, but I still wasn't selected for any international events.
Instead of protesting or making a formal complaint, I just
threw out my Sport Canada card and started receiving a
stipend from Israel.

Many racers thought I was a traitor—that I'd only switched
allegiances so I'd have a better shot at getting to the 2004
Athens Olympics. But Olympic riders are selected based
on how many points they accumulate throughout the season. And as mediocre as Canada was on the world stage,
Israel was even worse. I said nothing about Pierre publicly,
nor about my World Championship bike debacle. I really
couldn't. All I had was my point of view. No proof. No evidence that I'd been mistreated. My instincts told me to jump,
and I did. I announced that I'd have a better opportunity
with the Israeli team, and felt I had to switch. That's it.

Switching national allegiances doesn't change anything
about a cyclist's regular season. You could be French,
British, American—professional trade teams don't care

what your nationality is, as long as you win races for them. National teams assemble only for big races, like the Olympics, World Cup Races, or Pan Am Games. So even though my stipend would now come from Israel, I went right back to my American trade team and the North American National Racing Calendar (NRC).

OHIO

"Remembering you are going to die is the best way I know to avoid the trap of thinking you have something to lose. You are already naked. There is no reason not to follow your heart."

Steve Jobs

I got off my bike, laid it down on the pavement, and started walking back along the road. Connie and Rob quickly pulled the van over and ran toward me.

"Leah! Leah! Are you okay?" Connie yelled as she grabbed my elbow. I wobbled all over the place—I can only imagine what other motorists would've thought to see a Lycra-clad, sunburned, helmet-wearing lady weaving all over the side of the road, pulling on the braids at the back of her neck.

"I can't stand these anymore. My head hurts. And I saw a wallet."

Connie and Rob looked at each other and shrugged.

I took two more steps and picked it up. I handed the brown leather wallet to Connie, who looked relieved that I hadn't totally lost my mind, and turned back to my bike.

"We need to find who that belongs to. And we need to take the braids out," I repeated.

Connie picked my bike back up. "I promise I will find out whose wallet it is, but we have to leave the braids in. Your neck is toast."

I sighed.

At the end of the 2003 season, I overheard an opposing trade team director discussing the daily race plan with his cyclists. It was day three of a four-day stage race; I was in a porta-potty, and when I heard my name, my ears perked up.

"Yeah, but what about Goldstein," I heard a girl's voice say.

"Well, of course, she was good in the time trial yesterday, but she won't be a factor today. It's really hilly, and she can't climb worth shit," the director stated, just the same as if mentioning that the sky is blue and the grass is green. It's not good, bad, or otherwise. It just is.

I stood there for an extra moment, wondering why his words hit me so hard. *I don't care what people think about me! Why would that rattle me now?* I walked back to my team and grabbed my bike. We walked up to the starting line, the sound of shoes clipping into pedals making a background beat to the repeating words in my head. *Can't climb worth shit.*

Just as the gun went off, I figured it out. His words got to me for one reason: they were true. I was a great time trialist, but if I ever wanted to be a team leader—a GC rider—I would have to improve my climbing. And I knew the biggest step I'd have to take to get there. *Welcome back food obsession.*

Many cyclists chronically diet to sustain their slight frames. Only sprinters can afford extra mass, since they specialize in flatter, faster, and often one-day races. But throw in some big hills or multiple days, and a rider's strength-to-weight ratio becomes really important. Time trialists are right in the middle—sort of a sprinter, but usually less muscle mass. The French cyclists all joked that climbers are mountain goats, time trialists are horses, and sprinters are pigs.

I decided to lean down slightly over the winter.

I came back thinner and better in 2004, winning several B.C. Cup and French Cup races, the Lance Armstrong Time Trial in Philadelphia, and an eighth place finish at the Cascade Classic stage race. I'd accumulated enough points to compete in the August Athens Olympics, but instead of being excited, I started to dread it. In July, I stood at the starting line of Tour de Toona, the biggest stage race in North America. I'd finished sixth last year, and hoped to crack the podium this year. My Israeli teammate, Nicole Friedman, wheeled her bike up next to mine. We were on different trade teams for this race, but spoke briefly about the upcoming Olympic course.

"I heard the time trial course is really hilly," she pointed out. *Hills. Why is it always hills?*

"Yeah—someone already told me," I winced. I knew I couldn't podium, and, therefore, struggled to get excited about going.

Nicole laughed. "Don't worry so much. I'm sure it will work out fine."

"Sure," I answered. "Maybe I'll break my arm and I won't have to go."

With the sound of the gun, we clipped in, smiled, and waved. While I never broke my arm, I did manage to break my hand in a spectacular first-day crash that sent several girls to the hospital. Crashes are common in cycling—but I didn't *actually* plan to jinx myself. No Olympics for me. *Careful what you wish for.*

My season was over, so I immediately started preparing for the next year. I signed with Trek Red Truck's racing team and continued to drop weight. By the following summer, I'd won many B.C. cup races, the Columbia-Plateau Stage Race, and the Mount Hood Cycling Classic. My climbing was improving, my confidence growing. I asked Trek to send me to Cascade.

The 2005 Cascade Classic was a huge stage race in Oregon. The race was to be six stages and would include the compulsory prologue, time trial, road race, and crit (a multiple lap sprint race)—and I felt I could be a contender. Kristin Armstrong (U.S. National Champion) and Ina Teutenberg (prominent German sprinter), two of the top riders in the world, would be there, and I just couldn't resist testing myself against them.

Cascade was not on Trek's radar for that season, so I asked if I could go alone. Without a team, it's almost impossible to actually capture the overall win—but I thought I might at least win a stage. *And who knows?* Trek relented and paid my expenses to get there. The Pacific Northwest was perfect terrain to test my new, sleeker body. It's hilly—really hilly. Cascade was notoriously difficult, with long, grinding hills that never seem to end.

The opening stage started in Bend, and I have to say—I'm a fan. I love Oregon. The green scenery, the awesome hippy people, and the incredible riding make an irresistible combination for a cyclist like me. And, since I'm from Vancouver, the rain probably bothers me less than other visitors. I always get to races early, so like clockwork, I checked into the American Best Motel three days early.

Pulling into the driveway, I glanced up at their sign. It said, "Run by *Real* Americans." Great. I had to check into the "Prejudice Inn" and hope that their feelings for immigrant hotel owners didn't spill over onto Jewish cyclists. I never have understood why people have such strong opinions about immigrants—perhaps they've never heard their great-grandparents' stories?

The folks running the hotel turned out to be very nice, and by chance, cycling fans. They saw all my gear and immediately moved me to a room closer to the front of the hotel so they could keep an eye on my vehicle. They said they would watch my bikes too, and I had to stifle a laugh. I would never leave my bikes in a vehicle—not only would it be a huge financial loss (these bikes are crazy expensive), but I would lose my mind if I came all this way and couldn't race. And that's exactly what would happen if my bikes were stolen. So, into my cramped motel room they came. Just as with every race, I double-checked my gear including clothing, food, drinks, and every square inch of my bikes.

Many racers travel with just one bike, because of convenience or cost. Higher-level riders usually bring two to a multi-day stage race: a time trial and a road bike. By this stage in my career, I always traveled with three bikes—two road and one time trial. *Just in case.* Crashes are common and I always liked knowing I had a spare bike.

By 2005 and the Cascade Classic, I was already an established and respected rider. Cycling is definitely a hierarchy—and I had worked my way to the top of the pecking order. The night before the race, I spent my typical sleepless night visualizing each piece of the first stage. I had already driven the course and studied the sections where I knew the action would happen. Breakaways almost always happen on a climb, and I liked knowing where I could attack the group.

I had no teammates to help me, and I was nervous. I stared at my motel room ceiling and tried to feel the pain in my legs, the pace of my breathing, and see myself pulling away from the crowd. I'm sure I slept a bit that night—probably my normal four to five hours of tossing and turning.

The alarm buzzed at 5:00 a.m., but I was already awake. I went around and turned off my other three alarms, on my phone, watch, clock, and then called the front desk to cancel my wake-up call too. I'm a freak about being late, I admit it. I always set several alarms each night, but I actually rarely ever stay sleeping to hear one. I'm too paranoid. My body always wakes up early, "just in case." I loaded my bikes and gear into the car and headed to the starting line.

The first stage was a road race (about 100 km) with some significant climbing around Bend. I felt really good that day. I knew I was fit and I was ready to throw everything I had into this race. The riders milled around the waiting line, tight-lipped and edgy. The field has to wait about thirty yards back from the actual starting line while the race organizers call the hotshots up to the front. Usually the best ten riders in the field (national champions, stage race winners, etc.) get an introduction and then get to wheel their bike right up to the ribbon.

Everyone else must wait until the announcer says, "Rest of the field to the line" to make a hasty break for the best positions left. The back of the pack is brutal. To fight your way through the entire peloton, risking crashes, and begging riders to let you through is suicide.

Teutenberg, Armstrong, and I were all called to the front. I had met, raced, and spoken with many of the riders, but all we could manage was a brief greeting and a nod. This was business. And we all knew it. The ribbon was pulled to the side, and shortly after, the gun went off. We all clipped in and started falling into line. The start was fast and I took off with Teutenberg and Armstrong.

At the time, they were teammates with T-Mobile, one of the strongest teams in the world. Ina Teutenberg was a German National Champion, multiple stage race winner, and an exceptional sprinter. I honestly don't think I've ever seen her lose a flat race. She was and still is an incredibly talented rider—one of the best in the world. Kristin Armstrong was the U.S. National Champion, an up-and-coming star, gifted in her own right. They had each other to rely on and, therefore, had an advantage over me. But they knew I was strong and wouldn't take this race for granted. A team like T-Mobile was expected to win Cascade—the pressure was all on them.

The three of us churned away at the front for the first ten miles of flat riding. The contenders tend to push the pace at the beginning of a race, just to split up the peloton. The weaker and inexperienced riders drop back and form a secondary group. New riders are often unpredictable and have less-than-perfect bike-handling skills. Once they are dropped, the lead peloton is then safer and more organized. And that's just how cycling veterans like it, especially Ina who had a habit of straight-arming or outright slapping inferior riders.

In each stage, there are always races within the race. The first flat section is considered a sprint, along with several other fast legs. The overall fastest rider in these sections will get a "sprinter's jersey" at the end of the stage. There's also a climber's jersey, young rider's jersey, and perhaps a few others. Any jersey is great to throw on a resume to impress your sponsors, but the GC riders only really care about one—the overall leader's jersey. Teutenberg could win a sprint going backwards, so I just sat in with her and tried not to push the pace.

The first climb came around the twelve-mile mark, and the three of us made our move. Races are won on the climbs, and we set the pace fast enough to drop almost half of the front peloton. We had a few minutes of lead time on the main group as we crested the hill. About twelve riders remained in this lead pack out of the hundred or so we started with.

Teutenberg and Armstrong were definitely setting the pace, and all eyes were on them. They slowed slightly, and we settled back into a steady rhythm. I knew Teutenberg would go for the sprinter's jersey and Armstrong the climber's, but without a team, I couldn't afford to try for either. My only option was to sit in with them and try and save as much energy as possible. It was only a matter of time before they would start to test me and push my limits. Armstrong was an amazing climber, and I could tell she was shocked to see me sitting right on her wheel at the crest. She glanced at Teutenberg, with a silent "Oh, crap!" look. Teutenberg knew me from way back though—she smiled back at me and said, "Nice climb, Leah."

By the time we started any serious descending, some of the peloton had caught us again. I was a fearless downhill rider—having spent years racing in Europe with their insanely narrow roads and hairpin turns. Riders need virtually no skill to steer a bike down a hill in North America. The roads are wide and have gentle, easy turns. However, many U.S. races have a centerline rule, and this one was no exception. The rule states that a rider may not cross the yellow line on the road—limiting the shifting peloton to one lane. If an official sees you break this rule, you'll incur a two-minute penalty—an enormous amount of time in a race like this.

Now, bikes are not wide by any means. But even thirty riders jockeying for position in a twelve-foot space is tricky. We started our descent and started to pick up some serious speed, confident that our talented lead peloton would all hold their lines. We were about halfway down the hill, surging along at over 45 miles an hour, when it happened. A rider on my left crossed the centerline, and tried to quickly correct back into the peloton. Her body fell right into me ... and I knew my life would never be the same.

I had sort of lost count of how many times I thought I was going to die. Israeli Military, the Belush, and years of professional cycling had provided many opportunities to contemplate death. And as I was heading down toward the pavement, I was quite sure this might be it—my luck had run out. My face slammed into the pavement and I heard my teeth crack and snap. My body followed quickly after and the blacktop began burning off my clothes and skin.

I could feel bodies and bikes crushing down on me and I tried in vain to keep my face off the road. Again and again, falling riders pummeled me into the ground, as I slid uncontrollably down the highway. When I regained consciousness, I was lying face down in a pool of dark red blood. My left hand was close to my face and I hesitantly touched my mouth. I could feel a gaping hole above my teeth and my lips were hanging loose—nearly separated from my face .

Oh, my God—I'm going to be deformed forever. My brain quickly shifted to vital functions, although I could barely stay conscious let alone think clearly. I tried moving my legs, but nothing would happen. I saw that the tip of my index finger was nearly seared off, so I held that in place with my thumb and used my pinkie to hold up my lip. I could not see or feel my right arm at all. It had dislocated and was wrapped behind my neck.

I could hear screaming all around me. It was a huge heap of panic, and I was at the bottom of it. In all, about fifteen girls crashed and most of them needed medical attention. I must have looked the worst, because the "I think she's dead!" "Is she breathing?" "Nobody move her!" screams were pointed at me. My helmet, shoes, and most of my clothing had been ripped off. I knew my torso, thighs, and knees were beyond road-rashed and the blood was starting to pool around me.

Oddly, I didn't really feel any pain and I knew I was supposed to stay calm. It was difficult, believe me, with everyone around me losing their minds. I focused on my torn index finger and held it in place, hoping in some small way I was helping to keep my shattered body alive.

I went in and out of consciousness, but I remember someone coming to my head and saying she was a nurse. A small wave of relief went through me and I said, "I need help."

"Yes, I know," she said, "Help is on the way."

She tried to shade me from the blistering sun and her face was close to mine. Her face gave away her horror and again I felt a wave of fear.

"Am I going to die?" I whispered.

"No, you're not going to die," she replied.

But I could hear the edge of doubt in her voice. She tried to keep me talking, but all I could seem to ask was, "Are they here yet? When is help coming?"

She explained that there wasn't time to get an ambulance up here and that the helicopter was trying to find a landing spot. *Oh shit. This is worse than I thought.*

Waves of pain began invading, sweeping from my head

through my toes. I could feel the life starting to slip out of my body. Breathing was becoming so difficult; I wasn't sure how much longer I could suck air into my broken rib cage. I kept asking people to help me—I knew I was running out of time—and it seemed that help was taking forever. In all, I lay on the pavement for over an hour and a half. To me, it felt like two days.

Finally, the sound of the approaching helicopter came over the hill. It brought murmurs of relief from the crowd around me, but all it did to me was bring on a new surge of panic. My body was starting to scream in pain, and moving even an inch was excruciating. I totally lost it—in pure panic mode. I started begging the nurse not to let them touch me. She tried to reason with me. I needed a hospital, like now, and this was the fastest way there.

The blades from the chopper were deafening, but all I could hear was screaming—me—screaming—as the medics rolled what was left of me onto a stretcher. I remember feeling embarrassed. I'm not a screamer—or a drama queen. But the pain shot through my body like an electric current that wouldn't shut off. I yelled at them not to touch me, not move me. But, of course, they had to. And the torture of every tiny movement continued to assault me. The pain was incredible, and the screaming cycle continued all the way to the hospital. As the helicopter lifted off, I shut my eyes tight and wondered if death might just have been easier.

I saw eyes in the road. *Where are we? Kansas?* The little yellow balls shone out through the darkness, low to the ground. My imaginative brain created a body around it, and I instantly recognized a really short Mickey Mouse. *At least, it's not a monster this time.* Just then, a truck came over the hill in front of me and slammed into the back of Mickey. I heard a loud thump, the eyes disappeared, and I saw a ball of fur roll a few times. As I passed, I could make out the outline of a fox.

"Sorry you had to see that, Leah," Sean said over the radio. They all knew I liked animals almost more than people. They're so loyal, so utterly committed. I wasn't sure a human could come close.

Pennsylvania

*"Someone was hurt before you, wronged before you,
hungry before you, frightened before you, beaten before
you, humiliated before you, raped before you ... yet someone
survived ... you can do anything you choose to do."*
Maya Angelou

I heard the horn blare and glanced up just in time to
swerve around a head-on collision with a van. I locked
eyes with the screaming woman in the driver's seat,
instinctually leaned sharply to the right, and steadied
myself back in my own lane. The steep, windy descent
exaggerated my neck drop, and I had drifted into the
oncoming lane.

"Holy shit, Leah! Stay on the white line!" Lori yelled
through the radio.

I was too tired to respond. Too tired to be scared.
That'll seem scary next week.

"You okay?" Lori softened, and then laughed. "I think
that woman just pissed her pants!" We were all tired,
short-tempered, and slap-happy, and we could almost
taste the finish. The state line into Maryland loomed
ahead, pulling us toward the finish. *Almost there.* I nodded. *I almost peed my pants too.*

Mercifully, I fell unconscious sometime during my helicopter ride (the medics probably loaded me up with something) and I didn't open my eyes for about twenty-four
hours. I had to force my swollen eyes open and I blinked

into the bright light. There were about six people in the room—my father, sister, Danny (a family friend), and a few medical staff. My brain just couldn't compute what was going on. *Am I dreaming? Why are all these people here? Why am I in so much pain and why in the HELL can't I move my legs?*

My clothing had been cut away and I was lying face up on a stretcher. My open wounds were bandaged and I had already had operations on my shoulder and face. Slowly I started to piece the memory together. *Cascade Classic. Descending. Sliding. Hold tip of finger in place. Helicopter. Screaming.*

I looked at my sister and Danny—they were both ghost white. I could tell they wanted to say some reassuring words to me, but nothing would come out of their mouths.

My eyes darted to my father and we locked in a stare. He tried to hold it together, but I could see the tears in his eyes. I had never seen my father cry before, and it scared me. He made a joke about my modeling career and I could see the drops spill over his eyelids and down his cheeks. He quickly turned around and walked out of the room. My sister read me a few cards, including several from my Trek teammates wishing me well.

The next few days were a blur. I had scans, X-rays, tests, and several more surgeries on my mouth. My cheek, jaw, and the bone just along my eyebrow were broken. About 70 percent of my teeth were damaged, and my lips nearly ripped off. My right shoulder was dislocated and broken, along with my arm and several fingers. One ankle, along with most of my ribs, was fractured and my pelvis was shattered. My doctor, Carla Smith, had arranged a very talented plastic surgeon to tackle my face while she reset my shoulder and arm.

The first time we spoke she went over all my injuries and their plan for treatment. She was very concerned about my pelvis, and told me that I would need to get pins put in. I convinced her to wait a few days—I was terrified of having such an invasive surgery. It would almost certainly limit the use of my legs and, therefore, my athletic career. I could tell that no one really thought I'd ever walk straight again, let alone race a bike, but I knew deep down that I had to try. I wasn't done with cycling yet.

I hardly thought about my hips the first week or so, as the pain from the open wounds all down the front of my body took every ounce of strength I had. The nurses changed my bandages every three hours, and it took them an hour to do it. Needless to say, I got very little quality sleep. I could tell the staff was trying to be gentle with me, but the bandage-changing ritual was excruciating. On the third day, a nurse came in for my hourly check.

"How are you feeling?"

The intensifying pain made me shift side to side. "Not so good."

My morphine drip provided constant pain management, but the nurses gave me extra when necessary. I watched her turn the knob on the IV drip, and the clear liquid ran down the tube into the back of my hand. Almost immediately, I felt heavier. Not pain-free necessarily, but too stoned to care. The nurse walked out, just as I started reaching for the call button.

Something was wrong. My head listed to the side, and my chest felt like it was being crushed. I concentrated all of my effort on making my lungs expand and contract while I desperately fumbled for the call button. Black spots invaded my view of the ceiling. *Breathe, dammit. Oh shit, this is it.* I started saying goodbye to my family, one by one. My breaths grew shallower, my sight darker, when I finally pressed the button.

The nurse ran back in and looked at my vitals.

"Leah? Leah?" She took my pulse with her hand.

"I can't breathe. I can't breathe," I whispered. I could no longer see, and I felt an overwhelming sense of quiet release. If I was ready to die, I would've actually been relieved to feel so calm and happy at the end. But I really didn't want to die. Not at all. *Breathe, dammit.* I heard another nurse come into the room just before I passed out. I felt a mask get shoved onto my face, and the muffled voices slowly faded away.

When I opened my eyes, I was so happy I nearly cried. I was alive. I made it. I shifted myself to lift my head slightly, and reveled in the surge of pain from my head to my toes. *I am broken, but I am still here.* I pressed the call button, and I swear a nurse stood beside me before I'd released my thumb.

"I don't ever want morphine again."

The nurse nodded.

"And bring me a wheelchair."

She stared at me.

"I just want to move a little."

"Your physical therapist comes tomorrow. I think you'd better ask her." She left me a little cup of Demerol, my new painkiller, in little white pills. For the next week, I reminded every nurse and doctor that passed through my room that I don't take morphine. I never wanted to feel that sweet calm of death again.

Luckily, my therapist, M.J. Paulitz could roll with my crazy. From the first day, she taught the nurses and my sister how to get me in and out of the wheelchair. Our initial transition from bed to chair took at least thirty minutes, and by the time I had wheeled myself across the room with my one good foot and hand, an hour had gone by and I fell asleep sitting up. When I woke up, I wheeled myself back and they hoisted me back into bed.

And so the days went. Bandage change, transfer to chair, wheel into the hallway, fall asleep, roll back, and get back in bed. Repeat. Each day I could stay awake a little longer, survive the pain a little better, and make it down the hall a little further. The process was tedious, laborious, and excruciating—but I couldn't think of another way to start my comeback. One hand, one foot, and one roll at a time.

After two weeks, the Canadian medical system called and said that they missed me, and it was time to come home. Actually, they offered up a deadline on how many days they'd be willing to pay for my $3,000 per night hospital room, and that deadline was now. Carla thought I should be airlifted, but it would cost my family $10,000, so I opted for a four-day car ride with my sister. Between the bumps and cracks on Highway 5 and the twice-a-day bandage changes, I'm surprised I didn't jump out the window.

I spent two more weeks in a Vancouver hospital, and then moved into my parents' house to recover. And as I rolled into the hallway, I came face to face with myself in a full-length mirror. At the hospital, they had removed everything that would allow me to see my face. I knew they did it on purpose, but in the back of my mind I thought it really couldn't be that bad.

It was worse.

One side of my head was much bigger than the other; my lips were swollen out past my nose, covered in stitches and black bruises.

I'm not much for vanity, but that moment really set me back. I blinked back the tears as my mother cheerily wheeled me into the kitchen for some food. Always food. My father had built ramps all over their three-story house and, although that helped, the frustration of bumping into walls and sliding backward when I couldn't make it up one of them added to my irritation. The constant pain, and everyone trying to help me, coupled with my smashed face sent me further inside myself. I felt more alone and angrier than ever before.

Vancouver General did its own round of X-rays on my shoulder and hips. The surgeon shoved my initial pictures up next to his, and stood back. He swayed back and forth, as if double-checking his eyes.

"Well, I'm not exactly sure what to say here, Leah," he hesitated.

My mom and I looked at each other knowingly. *Yeah, we heal fast.*

"I can't believe it," he continued. "The break lines are barely visible. I've never seen hips heal like this. If this continues, I really doubt you'll need surgery."

I was relieved, but not overly surprised. I've always been convinced that movement makes bodies heal faster. Stress=Strength. Lying in a bed waiting to heal made no sense to me.

"Mom, take me to the track."

We drove to my old high school, Eric Hamber, and my mother helped me back into the wheelchair.

"You can leave me for an hour, Mom." The meeting with the doctor had given me a second wind. I started to believe in my comeback again. I felt my laser focus return.

"Okay. I will come back then." She left, but I knew she would just drive around the block and hide in the bushes. I didn't care. I needed some time alone—even if it was under surveillance.

I reached out my left foot, put my right hand on the wheel, and by pulling back my heel and pressing forward on my wrist, I started the two-inch-by-two-inch roll around the track. My shoulder, bound tightly to my body, throbbed from the movement, and I could feel the scabs on my burns stretch and break, but it felt so good to move, I didn't care a bit. I reached and pulled and sweated my way, bit by bit, along the smooth black surface. After an hour, I saw my mom's car emerge from around the corner. I'd completed one full lap.

My track workouts became the best time of my day, and each time I went just a little farther. Eventually, I built up to twenty laps, and then ditched my wheelchair for crutches. And as my wounds healed, I finally decided to get back on my bike. It was set up on a trainer, and I gingerly stepped onto the pedals and sat down. My one good arm supported most of my weight as I slowly turned the crank and reveled in the comforting, familiar whir of the wheel. *I think I can actually do this.*

As my shoulder healed, I started riding outside. Physically, I could feel my fitness returning—the strength building in my legs and my heart pounding with effort. I decided to ride up Cypress Mountain, a seven-mile climb, just to test myself. I was shocked at my speed, and then realized I was carrying about ten pounds less than pre-crash. Nothing spells weight loss like a hundred stitches in your lips. I half-smiled as I turned my bike to descend, but within twenty feet my hand unconsciously squeezed the brake.

What are you doing? Let it go! I chastised myself. The road wasn't really that steep. I used to scream down this hill at 50 mph, but now I could barely manage 20. Any faster and the crash flashed in front of me, just as real as the day it had happened. My heart pounded and fresh sweat slid down my face as I braked and braked and braked. I returned to my house and sat on the edge of my bed. I realized that I'd been braking while descending in my car too. *I need help. I need Tom.*

Tom Stewart was an ex-racer and coach from the Interior

of British Columbia. He had a reputation as a hard-ass—a coach who really pushed his riders' limits. Plus, he was an exceptional climber, and I knew I'd need to perfect that part of my racing if I was going to make a comeback.

At first, he balked. He was shocked to hear from me, and wasn't sure that I should really be trying to race again after such a horrific crash. I convinced him, and moved to Vernon.

The mountainous terrain of British Columbia provided the climbs, Tom provided the support, and my sore mouth kept me thin. Seasoned cyclists get it. Training, equipment, teammates, directors—all factors that separate good riders from great riders in the early stages of one's career—become less important at the elite level when everyone has these things. Carrying less weight on a bike, however, is a huge advantage in long stage races. Five pounds may not seem like much, but over many miles and many days, those pounds add up.

My slight frame flew up the hills, but my subconscious continued to balk coming back down.

"Leah, you know how to descend. You have the skill! Get off your brake!" Tom shouted next to me.

Even after we'd been training for months, and even though I'd improved, I still pulled the brakes a little too much. He'd told me that I didn't cause the crash, that I had to trust my skills and reminded me that there was absolutely no reason to climb a hill like a freight train and then descend it like a slug. He was right, of course. But the flashbacks continued.

By midwinter, however, I felt ready to race and started phoning teams. Each conversation transpired in a similar manner.

Leah: Hey (insert team director here), it's Leah Goldstein calling.

Director: Leah! Wow—how ARE you?

Leah: I'm great, actually. Back on my bike and looking for a team.

Silence.

Director: (stuttering). Well, I think that's just great. Good for you! We would love to have you, of course—but we've just filled our roster. Hey, good luck to ya!

That's it. I worked my way down to smaller Canadian teams, and even they didn't want me. Early that spring, my bike mechanic Ed listened to me complaining about my situation. He owned "Mighty Riders," a bike store in downtown Vancouver, and had worked with me on the National Team. He knew me. He listened to my rant, rolled his eyes, and then strolled into the back of his store. He came out with a jersey and threw it at me.

"Here! Go show them what you can do."

It was just a jersey. No bike, no shoes. But in that moment, that jersey meant more to me than any salary or fancy bike could have. It was a token, a reminder that someone still believed in me. That I wasn't crazy. I loved Ed for giving me that jersey, and I wore it with pride to my first solo race, which I won. And then I won another. And another. My fear of crashing into other riders pushed me from the gun; I'd take off and never look back.

Lead entire race and won Tour of White Rock.

Starting my comeback. Thanks for the jersey, Ed!

I raced the next two seasons with Canadian trade teams, and dominated most races I entered, winning Hatzic Valley Road Race, Enumclaw Stage Race, many B.C. Cup races, and the Israeli Nationals. And then the phone started to ring. And ring. Many of the teams that had turned me down before called and offered me bigger contracts than I'd ever had. But I still harbored resentment.

I raced with Symmetrics Canada that second year, a small, brand new women's team with a budget just big enough to get me back to Mt. Hood. I'd won the stage race two years in a row, and wanted to win it again. I only had one teammate, Marni Hambleton, and had managed to stay in the lead for the first four stages. The other top ten riders had teams of four, five, or even six riders to help them, but Marni and I had pushed to our max just to maintain the lead. She had done an amazing job pulling me this far, but I knew she was spent. I'd need help to win the next stage, the longest and hilliest section of the race.

I approached an ex-racer, Lisa Hunt, who was the current director of a modest U.S. team, Value Act Capital. The previous few seasons, they'd struggled to accumulate many points on the NRC circuit, and had no rider in contention for this race. I offered Lisa a cut of prize money if her team would help me win, an agreement common in bike racing. She agreed, and the team shocked me by staying with the front peloton, leading me out on breakaways, and sheltering me from the wind. It was as if suddenly they had a clear purpose, and they all rose to the challenge.

Coming back strong with Symmetrics Canada

I knew some of the riders, Martina Patella, Sharon Allpress, Hannah Banks, Katie Mactier, Courtenay Brown, and Taitt Sato. I'd been racing against them on the circuit, and knew they had individual talent. *Maybe they just need a leader. These girls know how to work.* The effort they put out both humbled and impressed me. I took first overall, and immediately asked Lisa about a contract.

"But, Leah, you know how small our budget is. I really couldn't afford to pay you much at all."

"I don't care. We'll make up for it in prize money." I really didn't care. I could feel the cohesion and the potential of the group and I wanted in. As long as the equipment was covered, I was happy. I didn't need money really, since I continued to work for David. I had something to prove and I didn't care how much money I made from it. *This little team is going big-time.*

Tom Stewart and I won every stage of the Tour Trans Alps.
I love Austria!

I was possessed. I can't say much of my cycling career felt "fun" exactly, but I enjoyed the challenge and savored the pain of pushing my physical limits. Before, I competed because I loved winning. The self-inflicted pressure and rigorous training schedule were torture for me, but seemed worth it if I succeeded. But now, I felt I had to compete for everyone who told me I couldn't. I started competing against a ghost—chasing me with fears of crashing, pressure to succeed, and running away from loneliness. All those emotions balled up into an obsession to win.

The 2008 Value Act Capital team, young and energetic, got swept up in my frenzy, and we started winning. A few riders left, and Lisa added Marni Hambleton, Nicole Evans, Lara Kroepsch, and Chrissy Ruiter. I was a GC rider, older and more experienced, and the girls responded to loftier goals. They no longer raced just to finish midpack. We raced to win. It was magic—we all worked for each other and suddenly riding my bike was actually fun and rewarding. I won several big races, including Mt. Hood again, the prestigious Tour of Gila, the Israel Nationals, Tour Trans Alps, Tour of Austria, and I set new climbing records on Mt. Seymour and Mt. Baker.

Our team became a team to watch, and over the winter, Value Act doubled our budget. Lisa, not agreeing with me about messing up the chemistry of the team, hired a few more top riders, Kristen McGrath and Robin Farina, instead of getting better equipment or increasing our salaries. I'd watched teams implode with too many big heads and not enough work ethic, and I feared that's what could happen to us. And although I could feel a slight shift in the harmony, we kept winning in 2009. Being the current champion of the Tour of Gila, I was asked to appear at a pre-race interview panel. I dreaded this type of attention, but all media is good for our sponsors and I couldn't refuse.

Five male riders and I sat up on a platform, TV cameras and microphones spread out in front of us.

I noticed there was one empty platform chair, and wondered if we were waiting for the most well-known cyclist in the world, Lance Armstrong. He'd won the Tour de France a record seven times between 1999 and 2005 with the U.S. Postal Service team. Everyone had buzzed about his new team, Radio Shack, competing in this race, and I assumed he'd be invited to the press event. I was right—they were expecting him. But he didn't show. Everyone waited fifteen minutes, and then thirty. Finally after forty-five minutes, they started the interviews without him. None of the riders were surprised. I didn't know Lance personally, but racing for as long as I had, I knew his reputation and racing personality. The guys all looked knowingly at each other. *Figures.*

As I headed back to my team (an hour late, thanks to Lance), a reporter stopped me and asked me a few more questions about the race and my background. Reporters always did this. They'd ask me more questions about kickboxing and Israeli commandos than about cycling. But I didn't mind, and happily answered his questions, right up until his final question.

"I guess someone like you would struggle to find someone great enough to look up to. I mean, who is your hero? Probably Lance, huh?"

I had to stifle a laugh. Why do people always look up to athletes? Just because someone can ride a bike fast doesn't make him superior or smarter or more respectable.

"Can't think of anyone except my mother," I replied simply, and walked away.

I gave my all and finished in a respectable fifth place. Later in the season, I won my Nationals again, and every B.C. Cup and time trial race I entered. By the end of the season, I knew I'd never repeat the previous two years. I had come back better than ever, and having nothing left to prove, quickly lost my motivation for professional racing. The team planned to bring in more big-name riders and I envisioned new personality problems and too much drama for me. I wasn't sure I wanted to continue another year.

Near the end of the season, I left the team for a few weeks to compete in my first ultra race, Furnace Creek 508—a 508-mile race in California, and I got hooked. An ultra-distance cycling race is any organized event beyond the usual and customary long-distance bike race. This is a fluid definition since the racecourse terrain, environmental conditions, and duration are three elements that define cycling "ultra"; however, most races are at least 300 miles long.

My rookie crew and I battled the worst winds in the history of the race, in which over half the field dropped out. The strong winds pushed riders off their bikes and I even got hit in the face by a wind-strewn scorpion! I ended up being the only woman to finish, and sixth among the men. Despite many mistakes and the worst saddle sore of my life (yes, even worse than during RAAM), I had found my next mountain to climb, my next obsession.

I'll ride one more year with Value Act, and then switch to ultra-distance and finally, the Race Across America.

I sat on the edge of the bed, in a crappy Eastern Pennsylvania motel, my mother offering me plates of scrambled eggs and homemade Russian dumplings. She'd brought her own hot plate and coolers of her homemade food. I felt awful that I could barely eat any of it.

I offered some to Connie, who gratefully accepted.

"Sick of ramen noodles and bagels?"

I smiled.

She rolled her eyes and nodded, popping a dumpling in her mouth. She rubbed cream on my feet (to prevent blisters) and pulled on my socks. *Wow—I must really be out of it. I've never let anyone touch my feet. Ever.* But today, the last day—I surrendered. And it felt good. Connie went out to review the plans for the final day with Ed and Sean, and Lori came in and sat down next to me.

"Ready to finish?"

"Yeah," I replied, stalling. "I gotta tell you something about this race, Lor. I figured something out."

"Really? What's that," she replied, not really expecting a clear thought to come out of my depleted brain.

"I hate racing my bike."

Maryland

"You hate racing your bike," Lori repeated, and then sarcastically shot back, "I think that's obvious—I mean, who else would sign up for a 3,000-mile bike race?"

I laughed. She had a point.

"No, really, I hate it. Remember a couple days ago when I rode through the thunderstorm?"

She nodded.

"I could see the lightning striking all around us, and the rain just poured down. Janessa and Ed tried to get me to pull off, but I didn't. I loved it. I found myself smiling so much I was almost laughing, and I started swerving just to hit the puddles—like kids do. It was so much fun. Maybe the first fun I've had on a bike since ... well, I don't know."

"So, maybe you're ready to retire," she replied.

"Yeah. Maybe." *But then who will I be?*

In early spring 2010, before our opening season training camp, Lisa called to tell me that the Value Act Capital team had been picked up by the Vera Bradley Foundation. Apparently, Value Act Capital could no longer sustain the large budget demanded by our team, and had dropped us. Vera Bradley Foundation, one of several breast cancer charities that were popping up everywhere, had snapped us up; they had one condition.

"We have to fundraise half our budget," Lisa explained, like it was no big deal.

"Huh? We have to raise our own budget?" I asked, confused.

The season hadn't even started, and I felt sick of cycling. My winter riding had felt tiresome and boring, and I dreaded training camp with too many egos and backroom drama. I had heard last season that several girls made separate deals with Lisa for extra equipment and gear, without being up front with everyone else. Of course, the rest of the girls found out. Chemistry, gone.

I knew the coming year would be more of the same, possibly worse. *Maybe I'm getting too old for this crap.* Not many women keep racing into their forties, not necessarily because they can't compete (in fact, I think many peak here, including me), but because they can't afford it anymore. Salaries are crap in women's cycling. If you're lucky, you may get travel expenses, two bikes and components, clothing, and a few other things from your sponsors. One year earlier in my career, our rice company sponsor gave everyone on the team a ten-pound supply. Rice, but no money.

And riders have a shot at prize money, but even that is notoriously slim, and must be split among many. Most professionals drop out to get "real" jobs and settle down. Many juggle jobs and racing, including me. But organizing specific pick-up and drop-off points with David was becoming a logistical nightmare. I would tell him my racing schedule, and he'd try and coordinate a job for me. The previous season, I had ridden first across a finish line in Washington. I had won a three-day stage race and the announcer and fans cheered my victory as I put my hand in the air. But instead of heading toward the podium, I continued accelerating toward my waiting truck, knowing I was running late for a pick up. I threw my bike in the back, pulled off my cycling shoes, and peeled out toward central California.

I couldn't even stay for the awards. I had to make some real money. Usually I'd pick up sealed documents or sometimes a bag in a train station locker or hidden behind a bench. I'd drop them in a similar manner at another location: New York, Minnesota, and all over the Pacific Northwest. I never looked at the sealed items. I didn't care in the least. My police days were over.

But I was still under contract with Vera Bradley. I was a professional cyclist. So I wearily checked in my bikes at the oversized baggage counter, and flew down to Redlands, California for the first race of the 2010 season. Vera Bradley reps had met us at our pre-season training camp, driving up in Cadillacs from their rooms at the Hilton, while we sat on plastic chairs outside our rooms at the Red Roof Inn. *Something stinks.*

The reps tried to rally us, and explain what great things we could all do together to combat breast cancer. But I couldn't take my eyes off their manicured fingers dripping with jewelry and designer shoes and clothing, alluding to their obviously huge expense accounts. *I'm going to ask people for money ... for this? Not gonna happen.* I rode with the team for a few more days, told Lisa I had to get home and there was no bloody way I would fundraise for those people, and left training camp early.

Lisa assured me that I wouldn't have to fundraise much, just show up and win the races that I could. I kept my feelings about the charity work to myself, but my teammates could sense my shift. A few days before Redlands started, Robin pulled me aside. She was another very experienced rider, and we'd been racing together for a couple of years.

"Everyone knows you don't want to be here, Leah." It was harsh, but necessary. "Your heart isn't in it anymore. Just move on—you don't need this. You know you want to be racing ultra-distance—you're a perfect fit, crazy girl."

She was right. I warmed up before the start of Stage 1, pedaling down a blocked-off side street thinking about what she said. *Why am I even hesitating? Just quit!* But I felt an ownership of this team—that I had helped build it, and should still care about it. But I had to admit I didn't. I was done. *I will announce my retirement after this race. That's it.* I felt relief; a new motivation. I sprinted along the warm-up course, and felt a hundred pounds lighter. For a moment.

I heard a car engine roaring to my left and I glanced up. *This is a closed road?* A woman drove past the warning signs doing about 40 mph, her head down (I believe texting), and before I could react, slammed into my back wheel. I was riding fast, too, and the impact ejected me twenty feet across the intersection. I was in the air forever; long enough to think: *Oh shit, here I go again.*

I came down face first, and fearing for my already battered head and teeth, I put my arms out to break my fall. I heard both of them snap right before my face smashed into the pavement. I writhed around on the pavement like a crazy person, trying not to look at the bones sticking out of my arms. I begged people for Advil (yes, crazy person) until the ambulance came and carted me away. I had three surgeries within forty-eight hours, and with plates and screws the doctors pieced my arms back together. My cheek was broken and my eye swelled shut. *It's just as well. I'd rather not look anyway.*

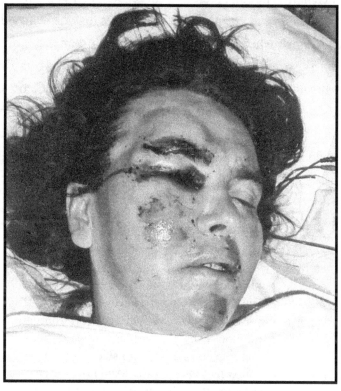

Me versus car bumper. Car won.

My mother flew down and drove me home. She moved in with me and became my full-time nurse. She did everything for me, and I mean everything. I had two completely non-functional arms; how could she not? By the time I'd gotten back to Vancouver, a teammate had emailed me asking how I was and telling me that I'd already been replaced with Anne Samplonius. *It's a small cycling world.* Another email from Lisa wished me well, and asked me to send back the team's disc wheel.

I took three hours to type her a terse email back. Holding a pencil in my mouth, I tediously clicked key after key—swearing, deleting, and sweating. I informed her that the team still had MY disc wheel, which was more valuable than theirs, and that I'd also like IT back. *I'm just cattle. After all these years, I'm replaceable in forty-eight hours.* I must've looked pathetic to my sister, who brought me tea with a straw as I slammed my pencil into the keyboard. My anger quickly turned to resolve. I could start ultra-training now. I didn't have to wait another year.

> *I can't believe I was so excited about ultra-racing back then. Right now, I can't believe anyone would do this shit on purpose.* My head and neck, beyond painful, felt disconnected from my body. *I wish.* The crew had started drawing mileage countdowns on the pavement. *100 miles to go! 75 miles to go!* The chalk drawings had evolved from practical, with big arrows showing me where to turn through the desert and mountains, to hilarious, with stick figure drawings doing all sorts of unmentionable things, breaking up the monotony of the prairies. And now, the chalk had returned to count us down; to get us to the finish

line. And no one wanted to be done more than me.

"Almost there, Leah," Connie encouraged.

No longer could I acknowledge them with a nod, and the call back button on my jersey seemed a really long way away from my hand. I flicked my thumb up. I couldn't manage anything else.

Unlike professional racing, ultra-distance cycling requires slightly different talents, like performing on little sleep, recovering quickly after hard efforts, and simply surviving discomfort for long periods. It was my calling. As a pro, the longer or hillier a race got, the better I'd perform. And unlike NRC racing, this was a sport I KNEW I could dominate, even if I had to start my training with broken arms.

I set my trainer up with two ironing boards beside my bike and started riding. My mom would have to help me on and off the bike, but once situated with resting arms, I could pedal for hours. Not fazed in the slightest, my mother would wedge a water bottle in the handlebars and go pull out the vacuum.

I showed up at the July 2010 Race Across Oregon feeling fit, although my arms still ached when I pulled my brakes or shifted gears. The 500-mile race served as a qualifying race for RAAM, so if I wanted to race RAAM next year, I had to get at least one shorter distance event under my belt this year. My crew and I, a bit more prepared than a year ago at Furnace Creek, hammered away to win it in just under forty hours. Race Across Oregon officially qualified me for RAAM, but wanting more experience I returned to Oregon a month later for a twenty-four-hour race called the Ring of Fire. The winner is determined by how far a rider goes within that time frame, and starts with a long out and back ride and finishes with 25-mile loops until the time runs out. I won that too, and set a new women's record.

I took one week off and then started the most grueling training year of my life. My food, laundry, thoughts, and days filled with Race Across America. I'd ride the trainer from 3:00 a.m. until 8:00 a.m., eat quickly, change my clothes, and head out on the road for another six to seven hours. Through the unusually bitter winter, I often rode my indoor trainer for upwards of ten hours at a stretch. Before going to sleep, I'd lay out four sets of cycling clothes, cut up energy bars, bags of cut fruit, make a dozen bottles of nutrient drinks, throw in a load of laundry, and check my bikes.

Early the next morning, I'd start on my TT bike, tucked into sleek position pedaling against an imaginary foe. If the weather cooperated, I'd switch to my road bike and climb up to our local ski hill, Silver Star, a few times. At the end of one such long, arduous day, I decided to finish off my ten-hour ride with one more climb; a steep three-mile incline common around my home in the Monashee Mountains. I struggled, standing on the pedals and pulling on the handlebars. A young guy pulled up beside me in a pro kit (cycling clothing showing your team sponsors) and glanced over. His shaved muscular legs gleamed in the sun; his face fresh and energetic. *Great. A hotshot.*

I was going to ignore him, and let him breeze past me

to the top. But before he broke away, he mumbled, "Atta girl!" smiled, and slid in front of me. Call it immature, but I just couldn't let that go. *Condescending little shithead.* My reserves flooded to my legs and I pounded after him, ignoring the screaming fatigue in my quads. I blew by him several hundred meters from the top, and didn't even look over at him. I victoriously turned at the top and sped by him as he strained his neck to see my jersey. I'm sure he was wondering who in the hell that old lady was.

I'd pedal for ten-, fourteen-, even a few twenty-hour days. I consulted with a few RAAM veterans, who assured me that I was overtraining. But I didn't agree, and just went longer. My old friends at Trek Red Truck agreed to sponsor me throughout my ultra-crazy phase, and gave me top-end frames. Shimano and Pearl Izumi stepped up big-time, supplying me with the best components available and cycling clothes that felt like silk. Zeal Optics sent an amazing amount of eyewear and shirts for the crew.

I was overwhelmingly grateful for the support. I showed up at the starting line of RAAM with great gear and a fun, energetic crew. I tried to enjoy the atmosphere, and be excited with the crew, but I felt the old familiar pressure sink onto my shoulders. *I have to break the record. These sponsors expect me to break the record. Everyone is counting on me to do it.*

As the days went on, and I realized the record was out of reach, I suddenly began to question my motives. *Why is this so damn important? Other people do this stuff for fun—why can't I?* I thought back to kickboxing, and how much I enjoyed the training and fighting. But since then, the military, police, and cycling had all been jobs. I felt compelled to continue them, until I'd reach the absolute top of my abilities, regardless of whether they were necessarily enjoyable.

I'd become the "crazy girl," with everyone wondering what I'd do next and some part of me felt that I needed to keep that up. I didn't regret anything I'd done—I'd experienced things most people only dream of, and those experiences shaped who I was, and who I was becoming. I looked back on my life accomplishments with gratitude, but something in me had shifted. I wanted more. And less.

"You did it, Leah!" Janessa hugged me at RAAM's Annapolis finish line, the huge Naval Base looming in the background. Dozens of people still hung around the waterfront even though it was past 9:00 p.m.

My mother and father's faces exposed their relief. I'd made it—with a gimpy neck, sunburn, saddle sores, but no major maladies. I wondered how many more years I could keep stressing them like this.

"Congratulations, Leah." My parents hugged me and the rest of the crew surrounded me, the eleven days of tension slowly sliding away. They all hugged each other, while the announcer called me to the stage. Janessa helped me up the stairs and, strangely, I felt nothing. George presented me with the trophy and asked me details about the race, and I robotically answered.

A VeloNews reporter asked me for an interview, and I had to call my crew in to explain the Shermer's Neck solution they'd come up with. She wrote all about the tape and the braids, and I secretly hoped she'd write more about that than my race. The *New York Times* and CBC phoned me for the story, and heartily congratulated me.

But I couldn't shake my disappointment at not breaking the record.

"You *won* Race Across America, Leah." Lori continued to point out the next day as we removed race numbers and sponsor posters from our rental van. "You also won Queen of the Mountains, Queen of the Prairies, and Rookie of the Year." Those were all the races within the race—fastest through the hilly sections, etc.

"I know. I just feel way too good. I should be destroyed right now—if I actually raced the damn thing."

"You missed a spot," Connie said, pointing at a piece of tape. "Maybe next year. We learned a lot."

"Yeah, maybe."

We obsessively scrubbed the vehicle and removed any trace of RAAM. The crew had rented the van in Washington on their way down to the starting line. We were in Ohio when someone read the fine print on the agreement and realized we weren't allowed to take it outside of the Pacific Northwest. *Oops.* We joked about how we would explain 10,000 miles in less than thirty days.

While I'd trained for RAAM, I had worked as a fitness trainer and coached a few local athletes. I found that when they broke a personal best, or lost a few inches, I was ecstatic. I was happier for them than I ever was for myself. The morning after RAAM, a client called to tell me she had won her age group in a local triathlon. I jumped on the bed with happiness—a far cry from my small smile and wave I'd done getting my trophy the night before.

I wanted other people to feel the joy of competing—not necessarily in a race, but with life. I started telling my story—to women's groups, high-risk teens, and corporations. Peoples' reactions shocked me, as they thanked me for reigniting their inner flame. I saw tears of understanding as I spoke about hospitals and rehab, and knowing nods as I admitted feelings of loneliness and fear. I felt a connection—a satisfaction deep in my soul that had been empty for years.

I felt myself softening and allowing people to actually get to know me. The real me. I started trusting more, and fearing less. As I heard people's stories and opinions, I had to admit that there are more good people than bad in this world. That there's more honesty than lies. And maybe, just maybe, more love than hate.

The truth is we all have fears that slow us down and doubts that speak louder than courage. I constantly hear people say things like, "Oh, I could never run 10 miles." or "I can't ride my bike that far!" And then I ask them why? "I have bad knees, my left leg is shorter than my right leg, I don't have time, my shoelaces aren't quite right." I've heard them all. But really what they mean is, "I'm scared. I'm afraid to try and fail. I'm afraid that if I succeed, then my excuses are no longer valid. I'm afraid of the unknown." And so I tell them, "I don't care. Do it anyway."

In my mind, you're either in the game of life or you're sitting on the bench! My mission is to convince people that the game is worth playing, regardless of your forty-page list of excuses. Take chances, push your boundaries, and trust your inner voice—it's worth the scrapes and disappointments! Trust me, victory is sweetest when you have scars on your knees.

Epilogue

I felt at peace with my new decision to leave cycling behind and start my next project. *I'm going to write a book.* I returned to B.C. and started looking for a writer while I rehabbed my neck. I kept it taped for weeks afterward, the weakness slow to heal. A couple weeks later, George the race director called to see how I was doing. Or so I thought.

"How's the neck, Leah?"

"It's okay—not sure if I'll ever be able to do that one again," I joked, not really.

"I'm sure it'll be fine. Listen, I have an interesting situation this summer at Race Across Oregon. I have three ex-RAAM champions competing, including the record holder, Seana Hogan. If you came, that would make it four! Epic! Plus, I don't think we've ever had a rider win RAAM and RAO in the same year ... could be you!"

I knew the powerhouse line-up was good for his race, and that's really why he called. The race was three weeks away. The wheels in my head started turning. *My legs are still good, since I didn't really race RAAM, I had merely ridden it. I could put all that training into another day, and actually push myself to my limits!*

"I'll think about it," I lied.

I went to my doctor, an orthopedic specialist named Gavin Smart.

"Will I have permanent neck damage if I race again so soon?"

"I can't really compare you to other people—you recover so fast." He was a recreational cyclist who had followed my career. "Besides, I know you'll do it anyway, so just go and do it. Keep it taped, though!"

I love my doctor.

My crew taped up my neck, stocked my coolers, and I rolled to the starting line itching to go. *This just might be fun.* I flew off the starting line and never looked back. I pushed myself so hard, I won by over three hours and set a new women's record. I still felt great, so I signed up for Ring of Fire right then. The next month, I raced so hard at ROF that I lapped the field and set a new *men's* record. And then, I felt satisfied. At the fittest I'd ever been in my forty-three years, I'd handily won three ultra-endurance races in one year.

"I'm retired," I said to George on the way out. "Don't call me anymore."

He nodded and smiled.

And then. *Why does there always have to be an "and then?"* A few local pros, who follow everything in the cycling world (I never have), started asking me if I'd heard what Seana Hogan had posted online.

"I don't give a crap," I lied to Sean, my riding buddy from way back.

"But she wrote a comment inferring that the only reason you won so many ultra races is because you weren't racing her!"

"Whatever. She dropped out of Race Across Oregon. She had her chance."

"But, she claims her follow car ran out of gas. Don't you REALLY want to beat her? She's doing Race Across the West (RAW) next year," he egged me on.

Seana holds the RAAM record. She's been THE best ultra cyclist in North America for years! Could I really beat her head to head? But what about slowing down? What about cutting down on the crazy stuff?

He raised his eyebrows at me. "It's only 800 miles."

Oh, shit.

I showed up at the RAW starting line seriously under-trained. I'd signed on the dotted line with my ego, but had no drive to put in the miles. Each morning I'd glare at my trainer and swear while I pulled on my shoes. I'd pedal for an eternity and glance at the clock. *Ten minutes. Oh. My. God.* For the first time in my life, I cut rides short. While training for RAAM, I lived by the clock—a ten-hour ride meant exactly ten hours. If I approached my driveway at nine hours and fifty-five minutes, I'd turn and ride the hill again. Insane? Maybe. But I believe that's what made me great.

This time, I'd write "ten-hour ride" in my journal, and then have to cross "ten" out and write "eight." I knew I hadn't done enough. I was going to have to race with my guts. Ego never helps turn the pedals. My crew and I stood at the sign-in table the morning before the race, when suddenly I felt my spine stiffen. The energy in the room changed and I glanced behind me. Seana had walked in.

She has won RAAM more times than any other woman, and holds multiple ultra-distance records. And she walked like it. She was fit; I could feel it. I let out a small whimper.

How in the hell am I going to pull this off? This will be the hardest race of my life.

From the gun, I tried to coach myself. *She is big and powerful—so fast on the flats. You may not be able to keep up with her.* My specialty, climbing, would hopefully save me once we hit the Rockies. The race—from Oceanside, California to Durango, Colorado—weaves through Death Valley, across the flats of Utah, and ends with enormous climbs into the mountains.

If I can just hang with her until then, I may be able to pull away.

I stayed on her tail until we hit the first long climb off the ocean. As I passed, she turned her head and spoke.

"I'll see you out there."

I believed her.

But for the first twelve hours, we never saw her. I rode alone at the front and slowly started to relax. *I was worried for nothing. I got this.* And then the radio crackled.

"Hey, Leah," Meshkat, one of my four-man crew, almost whispered. "She's coming up on you." *Oh, crap.*

Not only did she come up on me—she passed me like I was standing still. Seana pedaled a big gear, grinding her legs in a slow, powerful cadence. She was like a freight train. And I, spinning furiously, felt like a little insect caught in the breeze. Nevertheless, I found another gear and managed to keep her in sight. Sometime in the next few hours, I passed her. And then she passed me.

We leapfrogged each other for over twenty-four

hours—probably trading the lead ten times or more. Every time I'd stop to pee or change shorts, she'd charge by me and I'd spend the next hour chasing her down. It was exhausting and irritating, and each time I'd pass her she couldn't resist making a comment.

"You okay? Looks like you're not feeling so good." Crap like that. It was even more irritating, because she was right. I was working at threshold—a heart rate that I didn't know I'd be able to sustain for much longer.

I couldn't keep any food in me—vomiting and diarrhea plagued me for most of the first thirty hours. Early the second night, I had to stop. I pulled over and Meshkat grabbed my bike.

"I gotta sleep for a few minutes."

Meshkat and Lori laid me in the back of our van where I immediately fell asleep, and they watched as Seana and her follow car continued down the road. We had previously agreed that if I slept, it would be for fifteen minutes maximum, and then we'd continue. They left me for exactly fifteen and then pulled me back to my feet. I felt better. I still felt like I'd been racing my bike for two days, but at least I had shaken off the sleepiness and could continue.

I pushed off and clipped in, my cement legs resisting every turn. I willed them to pedal. *I gotta catch up again. Spin, you damn legs!* I stood up and tried to increase my speed. But I had to prepare myself. *Perhaps you're just going to have to lose. You can learn something from losing, right? Just finish as best as you can, and whatever happens, happens.* I blanked out for most of the night, and as the sun started to rise I pulled over. Lori ran up and caught my bike.

"I just want to take off my arm warmers—it's getting hot. How far ahead is she?" I mumbled, dreading the answer.

"You're ahead, Leah! You passed her hours ago!" My confused expression made her continue. "We radioed you when we passed her. She was pulled off, sleeping, I guess. You have about forty-five minutes on her."

I couldn't believe it. *How did I not hear that?* I ripped off my gloves and sleeves and grabbed my bike. I found a new depth of energy. *I have to get a lead that I can't lose, right now. I don't want to see a glimpse of her again.*

I put my head down and pushed myself as hard as I ever had, all the while promising myself that this would be the last one. *I swear legs—get me through this and I'll never torture you this badly again. You aren't going to let her catch us, are you? No.* And they responded. Over and over again, I coached myself through the waves of pain and over and over swearing I would never do this again.

As the hours ticked by, I put more and more time between us and, sure that we would win, we stopped briefly at a gas station. I sat beside Lisa and Lori and watched Gil, our fourth crewmember, put gas in the car.

"Déjà vu, huh, Leah?" Lori smiled.

"Yeah! Where's the cheering old guy when ya need him?"

"Git back on that bike, girl!" she laughed.

"No. I hate that bike. Don't ever let me do this shit again," I said, shaking my head.

"We both promise," Lisa interjected, "now get your ass back on that bike and finish. We want to go to bed."

I rode the big, last hill, often forgetting where I was, or

why I was riding my bike in the freezing cold. The crew took turns running beside me, cheering me on, and forcing me to continue. I rolled into Durango in the middle of the night, setting the new record by more than eight hours. When we went to the awards banquet the next day, Seana still hadn't finished. I ended up beating her by eleven hours.

I threw my ego into the ditch—I had nothing left to prove to anyone, and officially retired from cycling. The toughest races I'd ever done had also taught me the most. No regrets. Ever. But know when it's the end. Know when to put a period on the sentence and start a new chapter.

Afterwords

Afterword from Leah

FINALLY. This book has been a seven-year project. When I was first asked about writing a book, I honestly cringed at the idea of exposing my life to an open field. I am a very private person, so this was a huge leap for me.

Why then write it? I'm not exactly sure—but what I do know is that when I started speaking, many people would later come up to me, and express how I have inspired them, motivated them, and relit the fire that we all have burning inside. Some of us have a huge bonfire, but some of us seem to have only a flickering light that is slowly dying.

If my story is really that powerful and could potentially change someone's life, how could I not write a book? And although large crowds still make me a little uncomfortable, the high afterwards is well worth the extra gray hairs.

None of this would be possible without my writer, Lori Moger. Not only did she save my RAAM race, by shaving half my head and braiding tensor bandages into my hair (so I could finish looking like a bobblehead), but she also took on a project that I basically forced her into.

The year before I started training for RAAM, I came into work one day (I was working for Lori as one of her trainers) and walked into her office. I pulled out a tape recorder with about thirty hours' worth of recordings and told her,

"Hey, guess what? You're going to write a book. Thanks." And I quickly walked out.

It's not like she had lots of spare time—she was running her own fitness center, teaching boot camp classes, providing personal training, and carting around two very active kids. Her amazing children, Cameron and Halle are kind, inquisitive, outgoing and into so many sports, it makes my head roll. They probably spent many evenings asking their mother, "Are you done yet?" I'm so grateful to them for sharing their mom time with a computer. You guys rock!

Thank you, Lori from the bottom of my heart, for putting part of your life on hold for a project that you were "forced" into. You are truly awesome.

Thank you, my beautiful sister, Iris. You were more of a typical teenager than I was; sometimes it seemed we were more different than alike. Now I realize how difficult it may have been for you, to be the sister of someone like me. But you never showed any resentment or negativity—just supported me and always told me how proud you were. You even snuck a Christmas tree into our closet during my Jesus-phase! With you in my corner, I always felt protected and safe. I hope you always know how much that meant to me. You are the best sister in the world. I love you!

My father, who is one of the smartest, funniest, craziest people I know, created a strong foundation in me—a mindset that nothing is impossible. His determination to succeed, no matter what the situation, truly helped me break through barriers in my own life. He shakes his head at some of the nutty things I get into, but the truth is, I'm just like him. Thanks, I love you, Dad.

And finally, my best friend and constant supporter, my mother. It's very hard to explain our connection—as though her spirit, strength, and courage literally transferred themselves into my DNA. When I was a teenager, a cougar was spotted in Stanley Park, a large urban park in downtown Vancouver. Instead of staying away, as the authorities had suggested, my mother grabbed two flashlights and said, "Let's go find it!"

Yep—she's crazier than I am. I couldn't possibly list all the ways she's proven herself to be the best friend one could hope for. She is my rock and my best friend forever. Mom, I love you.

I'd also like to thank the numerous people who touched my life along the way. Due to numerous concussions (see previous pages), this list of names may not be accurate or complete! In fact, I have changed a few names to protect identities, but otherwise I have written this as close to my memories as possible.

From martial arts, thank you Mr. Choi (tae kwon do) and Alen Chang (kickboxing coach) for setting me up as a warrior for LIFE.

From my time in Israel, special thanks to Shahar (Krav Maga Commander); Yitzik Ingleman (Senior Sergeant Major, retired) and his amazing wife, Sima; Brigadier General Borovsky (retired); Yakov Turner (Police Commissioner, retired); Bosley (sorry I don't remember your real name, Head of Belush department); and Rami (Belush).

From professional cycling, Roger Sumner (coach), Sara Neil (coach), Barb Morris (coach), Steve Lund (coach), Sean Williams (training partner and pain in the butt), Neil Sawatzky and Peter Dorey (Olympia Cycle, Vernon), Jim Bates and Kyle and staff (Fresh Air, Kelowna), Greg Hammond and Elladee Brown (Shimano), Tara Lanes (Pearl Izumi), Mike Filinger (Zeal), Mike Hietpas (Trek), Tom Stewart (coach), Ed Luciano (Mighty Riders), Steve Born (Hammer Nutrition), Marni Hambleton (teammate), Nati Yam (Israel Team Director), Dr. Yoni (Israel Cycling Federation), Kevin Cunningham (Symetrics), Peter Kukula (Bianchi), Dr. Gavin Smart, M.J. Paulitz (physical therapist), and Dr. Twana Sparks. I've had too many directors, coaches, and teammates to possibly list them all—many thanks to the whole insane lot of ya!

I couldn't have survived RAAM and RAW without awesome crewmembers: Janessa Neufeld, Connie Cantrell, Lori Moger, Rob Martin, Ed Luciano, Sean Cameron, Roger Neufeld, Lisa Dorian, Meshkat Javid, and Gil Sneed. Huge thanks to all of you!

Big thanks to Linda Edgecomb for encouraging a banged-up athlete to open up in front of large groups of strangers.

AFTERWORD BY LORI

I'd really like to thank Leah for asking me to write this book for her, but I just can't. It was torture. I'm kidding, of course (mostly)! It was an honor to take this journey with you—thank you for trusting me and believing that a kinesiologist could actually play the part of a writer. You really are crazy.

Thank you to my amazing kids, Cameron and Halle, for being so understanding and encouraging. You two fill my heart every day. I SO love you!

Thanks to my parents, Bill and Bonnie Friend, and my sisters, Denise Bakker and Connie Cantrell (and their Mikes), for reading bits of chapters, giving your honest opinions, and believing in me.

Big thanks to all my buddies who helped proofread and give feedback: Zo Hogan (a dear friend and my high school English teacher who still loves red pen), Sabre Cherkowski (the fastest reader on the planet), and Debra Haldane, who told me to stick to my guns!

Afterword From Leah and Lori

A big thanks to Influence Publishing, especially editor Nina Shoroplova, who is a perfect blend of patient and direct, and Jeff and Heath at Sproing Creative and Dina Goldstein for their photography and creativity. Our sincere gratitude to Liz Stanley and Mary-Anne Morgan for sharing your artistic and imaginative talents!

Many thanks to Leah's aunts Udit, Ruti, and Ziva, and to Yitzik and General Borovsky for sharing your memories.

Thank you to Anne Samplonius for sharing your cycling knowledge with a clueless writer, and Clara Hughes for reading and believing.

And one last shout out to all the police and military personnel all over the world who put their lives in danger to create a more peaceful place for the rest of us. Regardless of politics, religion, or agendas, those men and women deserve our respect, honor, and thanks.

AUTHOR BIOGRAPHIES

Leah Goldstein

 Leah Goldstein is an internationally renowned athlete and speaker, who dares to push people past their perceived limits.

As a teenager she was a Tae Kwon Do and Kickboxing champion. She then served in the Israeli Military, training Elite Commandos and perfecting the art of pushing past physical limits. Leah then fought her way into a male-only special-ops police course and eventually into Israel's Undercover Police Unit.

The strain of anti-terrorist missions and confronting other violent crimes took its toll, and Leah found her salvation on a bike. Training tirelessly, she earned victories all over North America. A 2005 crash almost took her life, but she fought back by not only returning to professional cycling, but completing the most successful year of her career. Another crash in 2010 accelerated her decision to retire from the professional circuit. Switching to ultra-distance cycling, she had an undefeated, record breaking three-year stint, including a victory in the world's toughest bike race—Race Across America.

Today Leah shares her story and the lessons she has learned. Through discrimination, self-doubt, and missteps, she shows how astonishing achievements can be reached, one unflinching goal at a time.

Lori Moger

Lori Moger, M.Sc. is a Kinesiologist, Sports Psychologist, Writer, Speaker, and Fitness Coach. Her extensive background in wellness includes the Mayo Clinic Sports Medicine Center (Minnesota), The Sports Club Company (Los Angeles), and Indiana University's Sports Psychology Department. Lori's research about the physical and mental consequences of over-training has been published in *Medicine and Science in Sports and Exercise, Lifestyle Medicine,* and the *Mayo Clinic Proceedings.*

YOUR POSSIBILITIES ARE ENDLESS.

Further Information on the Authors

Co-Founders of No Finish Line Living

As Motivational and Wellness Speakers, Leah and Lori provide customizable keynotes and retreats dedicated to moving you into a healthy, purposeful life. As no-nonsense presenters, the No Finish Line team cuts through the noise and delivers the inspiration, perspiration, and information you need to achieve meaningful health—inside and out. Want serious motivation for you or your group? Bring in the team with over forty years combined experience in the wellness industry!

What We Do

Leah Goldstein

As a keynote motivational speaker, Leah shares her stunning story of determination, and encourages her audiences to burst through personal barriers and truly start living! She has inspired groups at many events, including the following:

- WOW (Women of Worth)
- International Association of Women Police
- Alberta Teachers' Association
- RCMP
- BC Corrections
- Alberta and B.C. Health Care Workers
- Plus numerous corporations and youth groups…

Lori Friend Moger, M.Sc.

Lori shares her no-magic-pill approach to fitness, food, and stress at corporate events, retreats, and seminars, including:

- WOW (Women of Worth)
- West Coast Women's Show
- TEC Canada
- BC Assessment
- Tolko Industries
- Community Futures

To book Leah and/or Lori for your next group event or find out where they are speaking next—you can find us! It's easy!!

www.nofinishlineliving.com
Facebook: No Finish Line Living
Twitter: @nofinishlineliv

See y'all at the next finish line…

CPSIA information can be obtained
at www.ICGtesting.com
Printed in the USA
BVHW070314211221
624506BV00019B/2088

9 780995 328402